Secrets of Short-handed
No Limit Hold'em

winning strategies for short-handed and heads up play

Danny Ashman

D&B
POKER SERIES

www.dandbpoker.com

First published in 2009 by D & B Publishing

British Library Cataloguing-in-Publication Data

A catalogue record for this book is available from the British Library.

ISBN: 978 1 904468 41 7

All sales enquiries should be directed to D&B Publishing:
Tel: 01273 711443, e-mail: info@dandbpoker.com,
Website: www.dandbpoker.com

Cover design by Horatio Monteverde.
Printed and bound in the UK by Clays, Bungay, Suffolk.

Contents

Introduction

Poker is a still new game

In 1998 internet poker began with the launch of the site Planet Poker. Not many people had heard of, or indeed played on, Planet Poker but it only took one more year until 1999 when the much bigger and successful Paradise Poker opened up for business. In 2001 Party-Poker started and this would later become the biggest site for online poker (before the government passed anti-gambling legislation in 2006). In 2003 Party's revenue was slightly over $100 million, but by 2005 it had peaked at well over $800 million. Even though it was big in 2003, it wasn't until as recently as 2005 that it really took off.

The same phenomenon of very recent growth has occurred in the arena of live poker. The World Series of Poker started in 1971 with a number of entries you could count on your fingers. By 2003 it had grown to 839 entries – a fair amount of growth, but that was as nothing compared to the next period of expansion where by 2006 there were 8,773 entries which amounted to a first place prize of $12,000,000 when Jamie Gold happened to win

Meanwhile the World Poker Tour scheduled a full twenty $10,000 tournaments for its season six schedule of 2007. All of these live tournaments go out on TV with the recent additions of poker shows such as *High Stakes Poker*, *Celebrity Poker*, the *Professional Poker Tour* and so on. The numbers do not lie and the facts cited above illustrate that though poker has existed for a long time, it has not existed in its current form – where it is orders of magnitude more popular and a part of popular culture – until very recently.

Because its new people don't understand it

All of this is of more than academic interest. Because poker is such a "new" game, the general level of understanding is quite low. Couple this with the following facts: a lot of people play poker and people play for a lot of money. Maybe the best word to describe the situation that exists is "opportunity" or perhaps two words that describe it even better are "tremendous opportunity".

This popularity has led to the increasing inclusion of poker in popular culture – for instance a $10,000,000 poker tournament was used as the setting for the James Bond movie *Casino Royale*. In this film, Bond's arch enemy Le Chiffre declares "All in. I have two pair and you have a 17.4% chance of making your straight", as if he has made a supposedly good play. According to conventional wisdom, this is apparently the math involved in the game – the type of skill required to play in a ten million dollar tournament. Naturally, the reality is somewhat different.

Perhaps an even better example from *Casino Royale* is where Le Chiffre says, "You changed your shirt Mr. Bond. I hope our little game isn't causing you to perspire". Bond replies "A little. But I won't consider myself to be in trouble until I start weeping blood". Bond has apparently picks up a "tell" on Le Chiffre that when he cries blood it gives away information about his hand. However the underlying idea is that the key to psychology in poker is looking at a person's face and figuring out what they have. Again, the reality is somewhat different.

For example, if in a baseball movie if someone said "Okay Slugger, you have big muscles on your arms. Use those to hit that ball far, real far and then we can win the game" this would be analogous to the *Casino Royale* dialogue about poker. The difference is that people take the *Casino Royale* dialogue more seriously but would realise that the comparable baseball dialogue is nonsense because baseball has been in popular culture for a comparatively long time.

If the skills cited by Bond and Le Chiffre were the true skills needed to master poker, they are so basic that everyone could be a poker expert in a couple of weeks. It is true that the two keystones to poker are psychology and math but those two terms actually mean something much more profound than most people think. This will be explained in great detail in this book.

There is a lot of money in poker

Before people could play poker online, they played in casinos. The best poker room in Las Vegas is the Bellagio and they have one room which seats a maximum of ten players. It should therefore be obvious that – compared to the action they can get by dealing blackjack or roulette – poker was not an attractive proposition for the casinos. This is part of the reason why poker has not been more popular in the past – it is not very profitable for the casinos. However, nowadays, thanks to the online revolution, a lot of people play poker.

Going back in time a few years, $2/$4 No Limit Hold'em (NLHE) was considered "high stakes" and there was not much action available online any higher. Slowly, and with some reluctance, sites added newer and higher stakes games that, at the time, caused great excitement among the players. The availability of $5/$10 NLHE games was a big deal, and then later when $10/$20 NLHE was added that was a big deal too.

As late as December of 2005 I emailed PokerStars Cardroom manager Lee Jones making the case for adding $25/$50 NLHE games. He responded, "No, I'm afraid we're not going to deploy bigger no limit hold'em games any time soon … that's not carved in stone (nothing in this business is) but unless I see a major shift that I'm not expecting, we won't be doing it." However since then they have added $25/$50 and then even $100/$200 and $200/$400 NLHE in addition.

The second most popular poker site is Full Tilt Poker. What makes them special is that they have the highest stakes poker games available. They host $1,000/$2,000 mixed limit games, $1,000/$2,000 LHE, along with $300/$600 Pot Limit Omaha (PLO) and $500/1,000 NLHE. Clearly therefore there is a huge amount of money involved – and it will pay massive dividends if you can learn to play it well.

Why this book will make you money

This book is ideal for someone who truly wants to understand poker. The reason this is the case is because I am a poker professional and I have put a lot of time and energy into putting everything I know into it. Many books are written by charlatans who have no right to be writing instructional material on poker (I call them charlatans because they are mediocre players). Most people who *could* write worthwhile things about poker don't bother. Most people who are qualified to write about poker and do are lazy. This book took a lot of work because it is a textbook on a new area of poker that has never been thoroughly examined.

First and foremost I am a professional poker player. I started out with $1,500 to my name and built that up by consistently ratcheting up my win rate. My wins come from consistent successes in cash games – I have never made a big tournament score. Tournaments require a lot of luck to succeed (granted skill too, but relative to cash games much less). It wouldn't be truthful to say that any old fool could win a tournament but *just about* any old fool can. Winning one tournament proves little about the skill of a player. Having numerous tournament successes does show something about a player's skill. However what shows the most about the skill level of a poker player is winning a lot over a long period of time in the highest stakes cash games. This wisdom is shown by the fact that I have never come close to going broke – in contrast to many poker players.

I have made most of my money playing $25/$50 NLHE heads-up which, when I was playing poker most seriously, was just about the biggest game offered. However along the way I have played a significant amount at higher stakes, up to $200/$400 NLHE and PLO, and also LHE up to the stakes $200/$400. I have played all these games live and online, shorthanded, heads-up (HU) and in full table formats. I have also played a fair amount of live $10,000 tournaments, although admittedly without much success. I've sat with over $100,000 in front of me playing poker with billionares, fools, and more skilled poker players than me. As a result of all that, I know a lot about poker, and everything I know is in this book.

About this book

My main game is high stakes NLHE, shorthanded and heads-up. As I go through topics like tilt, bankroll management and example hands they are all drawn from that context. However because all variants of poker are similar, the type of thinking and many of the concepts behind NLHE are very transferrable and helpful for all players – from micro stakes NLHE players to HU LHE players, tournament and even PLO players.

This book will not tell you precisely how to play poker. Instead it describes how I play poker and how I (and other top players) think when playing. The reason I have taken this approach is because it is impossible to create set rules on how to play or to give judgments on specific situations. *Indeed, some of the decisions, and even some of the logic I used could be wrong.* What is important are the concepts and ideas used to think through the poker. Poker is always situational, but once you understand the types of considerations that are important in decisions, coming to a decision itself becomes easier and only a matter of gaining experience.

This book is written for poker players with some experience of the game, not beginners. As such there will be no elementary explanations. Basic ideas such as pot odds will be explained quickly and through examples, and where this book differentiates from others is that the bulk of the book will comprise of taking those basic concepts and using them in advanced ways, as this is what high stakes NLHE is all about. Emphasis is placed on psychology and hand-reading. Hand reading and mental discipline are the two most important elements of poker. They are the focus of this book whereas most other books focus on "what line to take" (in other words the decision of whether to raise, fold or call) after the assumption is made that our hand-reading is correct. The "what line to take" decision is trivial and a matter of basic math when we know what our opponent's hand range is, so this book will focus primarily on the hand-reading element.

For the most part this book is not abstract essays on concepts in poker but instead a compilation of hands that actually happened. The type of thinking required to play the hand correctly and the ideas and concepts behind what happened are explained very specifically and in great detail. The ideas and complexity present in poker are not dumbed down in the least. Poker is a much better game that way.

Chapter One

Approaching the Game

The keys to winning poker

Poker is very competitive. Most of the traits needed to succeed in poker are derived from this fact and are, for the most part, similar to what is needed to succeed in other competitive endeavors (e.g. chess, soccer, racing). A good way to learn *how to learn* poker is to study how winners act and think – read biographies of winners. In this section the qualities needed to win are examined as they relate specifically to poker.

Passion for the game

The most important part of becoming a good poker player is having a passion for the game. Mozart said, "Neither a lofty degree of intelligence nor imagination nor both together go to the making of genius. Love, love, love, that is the soul of genius". You have to care about what you're doing to get really good at it. The concept of passion is slightly abstract, so let's try and make it more meaningful for a poker player. Since poker is, by its nature, very competitive, a passion for the game also means a desire to be the best player. Or put another way, it necessarily means a desire to beat everyone you play. When you are actually playing a real person this will translate into a desire to *crush* your opponent.. Incidentally, one of the best ways to gain or regain this passion is to watch players better than yourself and see them make really skillful plays – this can be inspiring.

The question is, how does someone achieve that high skill level where they are better than everyone else in their immediate environment? The answer is easy – it's the same answer a person would get that asked the same question regarding skill in any discipline – through hard work and study. But hardly anyone actually does that, instead they play poker and assume they'll get better as a result. They may do, but the process will be slow and erratic. Instead of playing poker and hoping that the side effect will be a gradual improvement, it's much better to act on our main goal and gear our plan specifically towards attaining this improvement.

If someone wants to be a doctor they don't just start doing surgery. They go to university for six years and intern for another two to study the profession. If someone wants to play soccer in the Premier League it takes many years of practice, practice and then some more practice. They study their discipline with professionalism. To succeed as a poker player is no different, this professionalism is needed.

Why poker is hard to learn

The difference between poker and other sports or professions is that, as previously discussed, it's a relatively new thing. There are no poker schools and there isn't much poker literature. There is no established roadmap for what it takes to become good. Everyone needs – to some extent – to go about reinventing the wheel. And it's not just learning how to play good poker, it's about learning how to *learn* how to play poker. And beyond that problem there are a few reasons unique to the discipline of poker that make it an especially hard game to master.

One reason is that for most of its history, poker has been played "live" with real cards. People didn't realize it until the invention of internet poker, but live poker was actually a very slow game. People get dealt maybe thirty hands an hour in live play. Compare this to an internet player playing two tables and getting one hundred hands an hour per table. The online player is getting almost seven times as many hands as the live player. This results in a lot more experience gained very quickly, so this player learns a lot faster. It takes a long time for a live player to learn the game since it takes so long to gain experience.

Then there is the fact that the best players don't teach, they play. The saying "those that can, do. And those that can't, teach" holds an element of truth. It is especially true in poker because the best poker players can make a lot of money. As a result the people that can make huge amounts of money logically decide to do just that. They concentrate their efforts on playing rather than teaching poker. Those that don't make huge amounts of money playing poker teach a lot more, because their opportunity cost isn't as high. When they are teaching instead of playing poker they aren't losing a lot because they don't make much money from poker in the first place.

Poker can also be very trying emotionally since it is so directly competitive and because money is such an integral part of the game. So if a player wants to learn and improve, they should disregard their emotions and use an analytical mind. However, it is actually quite hard to ignore your emotions. For example if a player wins a big pot, they should be calming their mind to analyze the hand and trying to understand if they played it correctly. When they do this they may realize that in fact they were outplayed and just got lucky. This would be an important part of the learning experience. However maybe the amount of money they won was substantial and, naturally, this makes them happy. So now they're celebrating and doing a little dance around the chair instead of thinking about the important things.

Conversely if a player makes a bad play and then the opponent capitalizes on it, maybe the person will become too depressed and beat themselves up with thoughts of "damn I'm so bad at poker. I'm just so bad at poker, why did I do that? I just lost $5,000. I'm so bad." Then they keep repeating this over and over in their head. Instead what they should be doing is getting rid of these negative emotions and quietly thinking over what went wrong, and how specifically the hand could have been played better. But it's quite hard to separate the emotional aspect of poker from the logical aspect which, inevitably, makes it hard for people to learn to play the game at a high level.

That brings us to the biggest reason poker is a hard game to learn. When learning takes place, a person will do something, and then he will receive feedback. The feedback – whether good or bad – is what people use to learn. For instance a student can do a math problem, but the key is when the teacher marks it as incorrect so the student will know to change how he approaches that problem. Or a teacher could mark it as correct, so the student will know to keep doing it the same way. That feedback is how a student adapts his behavior to be better.

Studying poker is a little like learning with a crazy math teacher. A teacher who marks problems right or wrong with no correlation to whether we did the problem correctly or not. The issue is that for a student of poker, the feedback is very difficult to interpret. For example, a player could play very badly, but win a lot of money. So the feedback is the exact opposite of what it should be. Here the experience merely reinforces the bad habits. Or a player could make a really good play and get unlucky and then think the good play was actually bad and not do it anymore. Again the feedback is all wrong.

There are many different ways this could happen – for instance a player could make a good play and get all the money in as a favorite and get outdrawn. The feedback is the opposite of what it should be, but it's pretty straightforward to understand that the play was good if the opponent hits a two-outer. However what if the player made what was in principle a good play but got called by a better hand

and ended up losing the pot as an underdog? Now the feedback is much more difficult to interpret.

Maybe one would normally expect the opponent to have a worse hand or maybe the normal outcome would be that the opponent would fold the better hand and it was just unlucky he called this particular time. Or there can be other possibilities – maybe the opponent shouldn't have had that hand in that situation and was lucky to have it there. It's quite difficult to "self check" the answer and evaluate one's play in poker because the feedback is so unreliable. Couple that with the emotional issues of playing the game and the lack of quality instructional material on poker, and it explains why most people face a lot of problems becoming skilled at the game.

In reality however, poker is actually a much simpler discipline to master than many others. For example, it takes a lifetime of good work to achieve top level skills as an actor, an artist, a soccer player, or perhaps as a writer. For a poker player it many only take a year or two to achieve a high level of skill. Although it is a complicated game, it's not nearly as complicated as other skills. It actually can be a lot easier to learn than people think – but when it doesn't the reason is usually because of these issues in learning.

Confidence and honesty

Confidence is fundamental in poker, as it is in all endeavors. It's also not just important for *learning* the game, but important for *playing* quality poker (this is discussed in the mental discipline section). A big part of the learning process takes place away from the table. This involves visualization and anticipating events that can occur. Imagine what would happen if you wanted to learn poker and so you thought about poker away from the table and visualized situations that might happen and how you would react to them, but then you lack the ingredient of confidence? You might be visualizing yourself getting into situations in the future and then playing them poorly. This is not what you want.

How can you be passionate about pursuing poker and becoming the best if you don't believe you are capable of doing it? It is nonsensical. With confidence that you have the ability to improve – coupled with the desire to improve – you will ask yourself the right questions. This will happen in specific game situations. Let's say you got outplayed in a pot but have confidence in yourself and your capabilities. The logical question for you to ask is "Okay I got outplayed in that hand. Let's see how I can play in a similar situation in the future to get better". Note that with confidence you will be feel secure and be able to be more honest with yourself and admit when someone outplayed you and so allow improvement to happen. However, if you do not have the confidence that you can beat this opponent then it makes no sense to try because, quite simply, you don't believe you can beat him in the future.

Also because of the difficulties discussed above in learning poker it is crucial that you are honest with yourself. Not only will lack of self-honesty hugely inhibit learning, but it will prevent accurate assessments of your own skill relative to your opponents. This will result in bad game selection. The reason honesty is so important is because, as we have seen, in poker feedback is so tricky to interpret. It's not like more straightforward pursuits where the results are clear cut and there is no way to hide from them, in poker one has to actively search for the truth.

A key to getting better at poker is brutal self-honesty. Do not allow yourself time to be satisfied with your play. If you lost a pot, see what you did wrong. And don't just look for a better line, look for the best line. Don't just consider whether you made a bad river call, consider whether the turn call was okay, consider whether pre-flop was okay, consider if your bet size was okay on the flop, consider if you should have bet 10% more. Consider everything.

If you won a pot because you got lucky, that's really the same as losing in the long run, so study that hand. If you won a pot because you outplayed the opponent that is not good enough – consider how you could have outplayed him even more. Consider if it just *looks* like you outplayed the opponent and in actuality you played it badly. Often players don't even know what hands to study because they think they played well when they actually played badly.

For this reason you should study a lot more hands than you think you should. A player often doesn't realize when they are making bad plays, or they simply wouldn't make them. Even if you are on the biggest upswing of your life you still need to study a lot of hands just as you would if the reverse were true. It pays to be tough on yourself and find as many mistakes in your play as you can. You'll be the one to benefit in the long run. The best plan is criticism of your own play, exposing the mistakes you make and then fixing them. Down the line this will pay off when you have improved by much more than everyone else because they have been complacent.

Why continual learning is important

As a poker player you are self-employed. There is no boss to decide when you get a raise. The only thing that decides when you get a raise is your skill level and the types of pay raises you can get are massive. There is huge upward mobility in poker. Win rates might start out at 1 cent an hour but the best players can make something like $5,000 an hour. Only a few people in the world are rewarded on that scale, although there are many players who can earn in the range of $1,000 an hour.

Because of this huge potential reward, it pays to focus extra hard on learning in poker. The best players put as much energy into learning as they can and their whole focus is on the future. The following saying is usually attributed to Abraham Lincoln, "If I had seven hours to chop a tree, I'd spend the first four sharpening my axe". It might appear as if some players who have had great success are naturally talented and did not need to study to get better. This is absolutely untrue. I guarantee that if you asked them you will find they studied the game one way or another. Maybe they didn't have a coach, or post on an internet forum, or do equity equations, but they did something. Whether that was talking to a friend about hands or even something as simple as thinking over poker in their heads in their own time. There is no short cut – a lot of hard work is required to get good at poker.

There are a couple of ways to approach poker. One is to play the game to make money. The other is to play to learn. It just so happens that if your approach involves learning to play better then, as a result, you just happen to make even more money than if your goal when sitting was to make money. And the difference will be significant – you will make *a lot* more money.

It makes sense in poker to take advantage of any resource that might help your game. This is because if you learn something new you don't get a $10 one-time bonus, instead you might make $10 more an hour for every hour of poker you play. The math is therefore that if you have to pay $100 for a poker lesson, and the coach teaches you just one little thing, then that is okay. Maybe that one little lesson only makes your expected win rate jump by $2 an hour. Then in that case you need to play 50 hours for it to pay off, and since you are a poker professional and poker is what you do you will play 50 more hours quite quickly. Everything after that is profit.

When I started playing poker I read literally everything I could get my hands on about the game. I bought a printer for the sole purpose of printing out five year old archives from a poker forum. I printed out over a thousand pages and read them all, and read all of the new content from the forum as well. I made friends with every poker player I could and asked as many questions as they would let me. I read every book that was available. When I played a session of poker I saved the hands and then after the session went over every hand thinking it through, deciding whether I got lucky or unlucky and if I played it well and how to play it better. I did equity equations on the hands and then when I was going to sleep thought over those same hands. I remember that after my initial introduction to poker – when I obsessed over it for a few months – I then took a break. However, towards the end of that break a couple of hands started popping into my head that I would continue to analyze and consider. It pays to completely immerse yourself in poker.

Another reason it pays to get really good at poker instead of just a little bit good is because the game is so stressful and because of the variance. Because it's so stressful it is hard to do as a fulltime job as well and this is not recommended unless you play really well. Let's consider a player who is quite good and makes $75 an hour. For some reason they start playing worse than normal and suddenly they are only making $35 an hour.

What will they do then? If they try playing more hours to make up for the lost win rate they may end up just playing even worse, self-destructing and losing money. Furthermore, since this player is just good and not great, they don't have a lot of money saved up in the bank and they get worried. So they play even more, get tired and keep losing. Now they can run into trouble. However, this is much less of a problem if this player is very good and makes $500 an hour. If they start losing, they have flexibility. They can drop down and still make $200 or $300 an hour and continue living very comfortably. They have more flexibility and thus less stress. The bottom is line is, the better you are the greater your flexibility.

Self-checking

Since poker is hard to think about objectively a good technique to use is to ask yourself questions. This will help your learning process immensely. When playing poker the first thing to do after a session is to examine the hands and decide who are the good players and who are the weaker ones. Don't consider whether you won or lost money – consider whether you played well or badly.

If you win a hand ask yourself if it was due to skill or luck. What would have happened in the hand if the cards were reversed? Say you had his hand and he had yours, would he have won as much money as you actually did? Would you have lost as much as he did? If you would have improved upon how he played and not lost as much, that shows you outplayed him and your skill was rewarded.

In reality it is rather more complicated than this because players don't all play the same style of poker at different skill levels. People play in different styles and with each different style comes different ways of making money. So, if you do the thought experiment and switch places with your opponent to find out if you would have fared better in their situation you need to be careful that it's not just because your playing styles are different. Maybe his style of play allows him to lose a bit more in a spot where you wouldn't have lost so much because he ends up making it back in other spots later on.

Another question to ask after the hand is over is "when did most of the money go in"? Did it go in when you were the favorite or the underdog? How big a favorite or underdog were you? Say some money went in when you were a favorite, but then some went in when you were an underdog. Then it is a math question – how much went in when you were a favorite and how much were you a favorite by; and how much went in when you were an underdog and how much of an underdog were you? What would have happened if your hand had remained good all the way – would the opponent have kept committing money like he did in the actual hand, or would he have stopped putting money into the pot if he hadn't hit his hand?

For example, let's say you win a hand because you called a turn bet with the plan of calling a river bluff, then the river card came and you called the river bet and won and that was a good play. Then let's say we did some basic analysis and figured out it was a profitable play when that river card came, but you need to go back and figure out what would have happened if other river cards had come and figure out if the play still works out profitable. Maybe your play was poor and the opponent was the unlucky one who just didn't get a good river card. Maybe his play would normally have worked. If you lost a hand the same type of analysis applies.

Naturally, analyzing a hand in this kind of depth can't be done during play. In fact, when facing a tough decision at the poker table you probably won't be able to figure it out in the 30 seconds or several minutes you might have under pressure. You just make the best decision you can from experience. The real learning will take place afterwards when you have hours to think it over. Then, when a similar situation arises in the future, you will have done the homework and be prepared to make the right decision. Similarly, you can't do equity equations at the table, but it helps enormously to do them away from the table. Play around with the numbers and see how important it is when you change certain factors and how it changes the play of the hand. Then, although you won't be able to do this math at the table for future hands you will be subconsciously estimating this math all the time and will find that your study away from the table has helped you enormously.

Intelligence

As you might imagine, intelligence is important in poker since is more competitive than most activities because people aren't just trying to win for the sake of winning – there is the additional element of money. Money is present in many mental activities, such as a prize in a chess tournament. However the relationship is not as direct as in poker. In poker the sole purpose is to win money. The only tool to accomplish this is by using your brain – it's against the rules to punch someone. And unlike other many activities there is no combination of mind and body, in poker it's just your mind.

There is an analogy here with sporting activities if we replace the use of brain for body. Take racing for example. There is a little bit of intelligence used to run a good race, but it is primarily about having a good body. In poker the body is of little importance – instead having a good mind is paramount. Of course skill and experience are also necessary. There are also activities, such as bowling, where experience is the key factor. Having a good body comes into play but compared to other sports not so much. "Technique" is what is important.

It's hard to say where exactly poker falls on this continuum but it is probably close to a game like soccer, since both skill and experience *and* a good mind are significant. In poker it is important to be constantly thinking and using your brain as much as you can. It is possible to play by shutting the brain off and going mainly on instinct (although this is still based on past experience). However your results will be poor. Use your head as much as you can in a poker game.

So, if that means you need to exercise or meditate before playing then do so. Using instinct for generic situations is okay but in short-handed play and HU play it will not be good enough because people quickly start adjusting to each other. For making adjustments to specific opponents and specific changes in the game that occur, conscious thinking through of the current situation is imperative.

However, this is not about mathematical intelligence, despite what many people think. The math element in poker is not how it is usually perceived. It is deep and underlies all poker hands, but the math is not advanced – it is simple algebra and statistics. Clear thinking is needed for that but it is not just the math that is important as psychology is necessary also. You need to outwit your opponent and to understand what he is thinking. Experience plays a part here for sure but every opponent is different so, on each occasion, you will have to think things through and come to an understanding of what your opponent is thinking, or how he is playing.

Chapter Two

Mental Discipline

General guidelines

We have seen that having a passion to improve is vital. Similarly, having a strong body and/or mind is also important. But mental discipline is perhaps the important trait in poker since when someone loses they actually lose their own money. This is quite a severe shock in contrast to what happens in other pursuits when someone fails. In an athletic or sporting event if someone messes up they lose, but the losses aren't penalized. That is the key – in most other competitive pursuits the loser is not actually penalized, instead the person's skill level stagnates in their activity.

But in poker when *you* mess up you lose *your* money. This is not stagnating, but going backwards, and it is a very bad result. This tends to affect the mind even more and the consequence can be further losses, which can and do break people emotionally and financially. Things are different in, say, soccer. If an aspiring college athlete does badly he doesn't go broke and his body won't self destruct. He may be disappointed but he won't go crazy. He'll stay in the same spot and not lose anything. He'll later either resume his march forward or quit the sport.

In poker, players often make informal rules to protect themselves from these negative penalties – to make it more of a safe activity like soccer so they can't really lose too much. With these rules they can then face the normal swings of variance, but those swings become expected. They might appear negative on the outside, but someone who understands will realise that they aren't too bad and are just part of the game. Absorbing these normal swings in variance is essential in order to gain in the long run in poker. In many activities consistent negative results would make it obvious that a person should concentrate their efforts elsewhere. However, in poker it is much more confusing because of unreliable feedback. This is why there are "rules" people make up to protect themselves.

When a person loses money following these rules (and everyone sets up their own based on whatever works best for them), they are regarded as normal business losses that are expected and not a problem. For instance if someone has a bankroll of $100,000 and tries playing $25/$50 NLHE that is completely reasonable providing that if they lose $15,000 they then drop back down to their regular game of $10/$25. Or if I am playing an opponent and he busts me for a buy-in and I realize he is better than me and stop that is also fine (of course it is better if I realize that sooner and quit). Those are normal unavoidable expenses of doing things like trying to improve in poker and make more money.

What is unacceptable though is when someone has $20,000 to their name, their only job is poker and they are playing $25/$50 NLHE. That is ridiculously unprofessional and such a person has little chance of success as they have no mental discipline. They probably know they shouldn't play that game but most likely they were losing earlier on and began chasing their losses. You need to be able to control your head, how you think and what you do when you play poker or you will go backward and maybe even end up on the street.

The rules that most people follow are discussed below and relate to issues of moving up in stakes, bankroll management and so on. But for now just know that you need the mental discipline to follow the guidelines you set for yourself, in order to allow yourself to play the best poker you can for as long you can.

Winning poker

Playing winning poker is about a couple of things. Firstly it's about playing your best, or as good as you can, for as long as you can play. And it's also about playing your worst as infrequently as you can. It is a bit misleading to use the word tilt as if there are two levels to play poker on – normal poker, and tilt poker. In fact, there is a huge variety in what poker game people bring to the table. Most people very rarely bring a 100% effort to the table. Most people play average, middling poker for most of the time with little periods of relative brilliance and stupidity thrown in.

When you start playing you should come into the game with the mindset that you want to crush your opponents. If you start out sloppy and lose from the outset you will spend your entire session trying to get even and your play will suffer. Start out by playing precise, winning poker and try to continue in that mindset throughout the game.

As we have already said, to play the best poker you can having a passion for the game is essential. One thing that could help is to watch better people play, remind yourself what you are striving to achieve, how much you want achieve it, see how great they play and remember you want to achieve the same. And remember to do what they do, and what you need to do, which is to play as best you can for as high a percentage of the time as you can.

Playing your best poker is also constructive in terms of learning and getting better. When your mind is focused 100% on trying to play your best and thinking everything over you will learn a lot more than when you play average poker (this works in the reverse too). When your main focus in poker is learning and getting better it forces you to put in maximum effort at the table which will help you learn and as a side effect you'll play better and win more money. In poker you should always keep the mindset that you are at the table playing poker to learn, to become even better and to move up in stakes – this is crucially important.

Tilt

Poker can be difficult on the psyche at times. Sometimes you will be playing good poker and you will still lose. Don't compound these situations by tilting and playing worse, and as a result losing more money. When you tilt because of bad luck it usually means that the money you are playing for means too much to you. There are a couple of explanations for this. One is that you only think about poker as a job and in terms of the money you make. You might be constantly worried about how much money you have won or lost in a session, always counting your chips or checking your bankroll. This is a bad habit that should be stopped. Look at poker as a game that you can try to master, not as a means to make money. When you are less concerned with wins and losses and more concerned with playing well, you will be less inclined to tilt.

Another explanation for why the money means too much to you is if you are playing higher stakes than you are used to. Higher stakes will increase the stress of playing because the potential win or loss will be greater than you are used to. If you are a player who has trouble playing under stressful conditions then it might not be a good idea to take shots at higher stakes. But, if you practice mental discipline then taking shots can help your game and your bankroll.

Another factor that may cause you to tilt is when you make a bad play. Poker is a long journey that will never be completed – you will always be changing your game and improving. Also, you will make many mistakes along the way, as all players do. So if you lose money by making a mistake you need to realize that in the grand scheme of things it doesn't matter. You are constantly learning to get better and one of the ways to learn is by evaluating your mistakes. If you see the reason you made a mistake and correct it then in the future than your game will benefit. Don't make the mistake worse by tilting afterwards.

The seven deadly sins

People tilt because of emotions, and some of the seven deadly sins come into play here. In fact they all do, to greater and lesser extents – the least important being lust which can for all practical purposes be excluded unless a pretty lady is watching and it compels you to make an "impressive" play to show her your skills. Similarly gluttony doesn't play much of a part in a poker player's downfall either under normal circumstances.

Anger is an interesting emotion in that unlike all the others it has a good chance of actually helping a player if it is directed at your opponents. If you win it's against a player you hate, and if you lose it's against a player you hate, so this will focus your efforts in a big way to make you do everything you can to win.

Pride and vanity come into play also and are related to the idea of honesty which, as discussed already, is very important. If a player is not honest with themselves they give in to vanity and pride and think themselves better than they really are. This can lead them to sit in games they shouldn't be playing. These are games where a player of the imagined skill level might be expected to earn more money, but – in actuality – our misguided hero will be expected to lose.

Envy can also lead a player to play stakes higher than they should to mimic and try to obtain what other players have. On the other hand it could serve as a driving force to make a player improve. Perhaps this could work, but even *Star Wars* made the point that if the powers acquired by the converting to the Dark Side are strong, they are not worth giving in to. So use negative emotions at your own risk.

Sloth is a serious problem for poker players too. Laziness will slow a player's learning greatly (as well as their win rate). Learning slowly takes a little hard work, and learning fast takes a lot of hard work. If a person puts in no hard work at all they will experience no learning. Again, learning is the key to success in poker so you have to be vigorous and energetic in its pursuit.

The other problem with laziness is that it will very directly make you win less money at the table. In almost all jobs people get lazy and even if their boss catches them the consequences might just be some sharp words. However in a way, poker has less luck involved than other professions – the cards do not lie and it is just simple math that rewards good play and punishes bad play over time. If you are lazy a little bit you will be punished a little over time, and if you are lazy a lot you will be punished a lot. The choice is yours.

The worst problem at the table is greed. Most people want money, and a lot of money as fast as they can get it. But that's not the way things work in poker – acting on your emotions and desires won't help. Just because at a given moment you are impatient to get more money or get it faster than you normally do, this doesn't mean you can act on this and get it. Greed needs to be pushed aside and ignored when playing poker.

For many people poker is simply a job. But unlike other jobs the pay isn't steady. In other jobs a person knows that for an hour worked, he will gain an expected amount in his paycheck. Poker is different and people can go on losing streaks for long periods of time.. This person might then think "well this sucks, I'm not playing poker for my health – I want my money now". This is greed since they want money immediately. But that's not the way poker works because that emotion will make them play worse and lose money. This is a good opportunity to gain an edge over your opponents because most people are very seriously affected by a long term downswing, so if you can be not affected much that will be a huge difference and thus a huge edge over your opponents.

Similarly, after a player has lost a good deal of money in a session sometimes he becomes focused on winning it back rather than playing good poker. When this happens a player becomes concentrated on winning a big pot and as a result plays bad poker. This is a critical mistake and will cause you to lose a lot of money.

For example, let's say you have Q-J, raise pre-flop and get called. Then you flop top pair and bet the flop and get called and then an inconsequential card comes on the turn. Now normally you'd check here to keep the pot medium sized with a modest hand such as top pair, medium kicker. But because you're down a buy-in and you want to win it back you bet the turn. If betting the turn here was correct, you would do it all the time. But it isn't because your hand isn't good enough to go all-in with and if your opponent raises you must fold and he won't call with a worse hand. Instead of winning your money back, you will lose more.

When you are only focused on winning big pots you neglect small pots. In short-handed play marginal situations arise frequently in small pots. It is a costly error to forfeit all the small pots because you are only concerned with winning a big pot. Most of the time big pots are just the result of luck, like pocket aces running into pocket kings. These kinds of hands will even out in the long run, so your advantage is outplaying your opponents in the smaller pots which will add up quickly. Also playing every hand and all the small pots well is crucial to frustrating the opposition. If your opponents have an easy time in the small pots they will feel relaxed and be playing well when the big pots arise. However, if you are really outplaying them and making them feel bad in every single hand they will become frustrated and play the big pots poorly. This last point is critical.

There are a few other traits that don't fit into the seven deadly sins that are worth discussing. Curiosity is present at the table a lot if you are playing good poker and trying to figure out what your opponents have. But when you reach the river and your opponent bets and you are curious what he has but you are pretty sure he has you beat that first reason should be ignored. Another problem that can arise is boredom. Boredom will lead to a lack of focus and a lack of thinking that will make you play worse. It could also lead to forcing the action to make things more exciting

The last of the problems that will be discussed here is desperation, or a lack of confidence. Maybe there has been a bad run of cards and for a while you simply cannot win. In psychology this is called "learned hopelessness" and it leads to people doing really stupid things even when history has taught them they cannot win. However in poker we know that unreliable feedback can sometimes teach you to do the wrong things. On long downswings, you should not give in to desperation or stop making plays that are normally good plays because in a recent unlucky streak they have appeared to be bad.

The importance of not tilting

As we have seen, tilt is a major factor in poker, and if you learn not to tilt you be able to progress as a player at a much faster rate. Of course, if you play $1/$2 NLH and eliminate tilt from your game you won't be able to jump right up to $5/$10. But, you won't have to spend hours and hours grinding away to try to make up for money you lose on tilt and you will progress faster.

Many people underestimate just how high a win rate is possible, and how much tilting can impact this. When playing heads-up online you can play 100-400 hands per hour, compared to full-ring live play where you are fortunate to get 20 to 30 hands per hour. You get so many more hands online that if you tilt for a short time you could cost yourself a great deal of money. Conversely, when you are playing well your win rate will be magnified because you are playing more hands.

If you are tilting and happen to lose a buy-in, think about how long it will take you to make it back. If you make ten big blinds an hour on average, it might take you ten hours of playing to make it up. Also, when you calculate your win rate of ten big blinds per hour that accounts for all the times you tilt away money. So if you play your best poker all the time your win rate would be significantly higher.

It is impossible to fully eradicate tilt. Even some of the best players in the world have massive tilt problems. They may have huge win rates, but sometimes tilt away five $10,000 dollar buy-ins in a session. If you can learn to play poker as well as some of the top players but not tilt imagine what kind of money you could be making!

When playing heads-up everything is also magnified – both your skill and tilt problems. Sometimes you may not be on tilt per se, but you may be not playing as well as normal. Maybe you're not concentrating sufficiently, are a little off your game, or playing listlessly because of boredom. But these mistakes will wreak similar havoc to tilt. When you are playing poorly or tilting it might be a good idea to quit the game.

This is an interesting point, because it's what most people advocate when you are tilting. However the decision is a little more complicated in the moment and it depends how good your mental discipline is. If you have good mental discipline it can pay off big-time to stay in the game assuming you have a good edge. The reason is that if you have been tilting and making crazy plays, your opponent will have noticed this and you will be in a good position to "change gears" and start playing solid poker to take advantage of a great table image.

How to avoid tilting

To be a successful player it is clearly imperative that you minimize tilt. Your winnings come from your opponents and this might be because you are you an amazing player, or an amazingly disciplined player. Of course the best thing to be is both, however if you had to choose one the correct answer would be disciplined. You won't have to deal with the enormous variance associated with huge wins and huge losses which will make poker much less stressful.

Take a step back and look where the money you are tilting away is going. It doesn't just disappear, it doesn't go to help a friend, buy a product, or to a deserving charity. It goes to your opponent – the enemy, the villain of the hands you play, the person you need to beat to be successful. When you think about losses in this way it might help you avoid tilt. And when you get the urge to make a bad play because you are frustrated or bored, think about how unhappy it will make you later on. There is no need to rush important decisions – take your time and really think it through. Be methodical about playing poker.

Another way to avoid tilt on downswings is not to get hung up on your current stack or bankroll and not worry about how much bigger they were previously. This train of thought will force you to play too aggressively in hopes of regaining what you once had. Sometimes your bankroll or stack will fluctuate downward but you must avoid giving into to greed when you are in one of these downswings since forcing the action will likely cause you to lose more money.

The journey of learning to play poker can often seem to take you two steps forward and one step back, but everyone who plays the game goes through long periods of losing at some point. This is often a combination of bad luck and also bad play, since when people start losing they invariably begin to play worse. However it is important to try to avoid long term tilt in order to minimize your losses.

Sometimes when you are on a bad streak of cards you start making thinner value bets and more bluffs in an attempt to recoup your losses. Other times your opponents might be on a good run of cards and when you play aggressively they keep showing up with big hands and this causes you to play scared. Long losing streaks are like fog in the distance – they cause you to lose your way on the journey.

There are generally two remedies for long term tilt. For some players, taking an extended break from the game might be a good idea. After long breaks the fog will subside and your mind will become clearer. Poker isn't a steady climb upwards – there are frequently valleys and plateaus encountered on the way.

For other players a better remedy might be to just refocus your efforts and force yourself to play your best poker. This will work better for players with stronger willpower. If you are playing good poker you will eventually win, so just ride out the losing streaks as there are greener pastures ahead.

Conversely there exists the problem of playing below your normal skill level, and note that such issues can compound themselves. When you play good, you will continue to play better and better and your opponent may play worse and worse. But when you play bad the opponent will play better and you will play worse yourself. This is why when you start playing bad and tilting it's hard to reverse the trend and it is usually better to just quit.

Empowering yourself

Many different things have been brought up so far that contribute to how good or bad a player will do in general in poker. However, rather than being overwhelmed by them you should view the possibilities as empowering. All of these elements are in your hands to do with as you choose. They are all very concrete ways to improve your poker game and gain an edge on your opponents. The fact that there are so many different aspects to poker, and varying degrees of skill means that the differences in win rates between players will be huge – and, assuming you are prepared to work hard, this is a very good thing as it means upward mobility and the potential for you to make a lot of money. However, these are just some of the underlying factors that will contribute to your success, and it is now time to move onto discussing the more concrete factors involved if winning at high stakes no limit hold'em.

Chapter Three

Strategic Considerations

Shorthanded vs. full table

A no limit hold'em game can be played with anywhere from two to ten players. The change from a two-handed to a full-ring game is gradual and continuous. With more players in the game, patience becomes a huge virtue. Because more players are involved, more hands are dealt so the winning hands are higher in quality, and therefore you simply have to wait for a good hand to play. As the game gets more shorthanded the hand strengths go down so it's less about waiting for a good hand and more about outplaying your opponents.

Obviously, in a ten-handed game – all other things being equal – you will win one in ten hands, but in a heads-up game you will win one in two. Thus you are competing over more pots. And because you are fighting over more pots many more decisions arise and people will be fighting for pots using more than just the value of their hands. Similarly, the more people at a table the more important it is to play straightforward poker because it will take a long time before your opponents adjust to your play, whereas the less people are at the table the more you need to mix it up and constantly adjust your play.

Live vs. online

Live poker and online poker are very different games. In live poker because everyone is only playing one table at a time, and because at that one table hands come much slower, individual hands have a greater importance. Online poker is more about developing a system of play that works and not worrying about individual hands as much. Live poker is about focusing on every hand and trying to win as many pots as possible. Seeing live players fighting for big pots with marginal hands demonstrates how rare big hands actually are. Also, live play shows that concentrating on playing every hand optimally leads to obtaining maximum value. Online, people often get bogged down in their "system" and lose some value by not concentrating on every hand and seeing the specific aspects.

For example, online a person playing five tables might see a situation as "I have top pair with a mediocre kicker, that is not good enough to play for 100 big blinds (BB) so I fold." That is playing on autopilot and it misses a lot of the specifics of a hand. In live play because there is only one table and limited distractions people are able to concentrate better which leads them to hand read better and develop a better understanding of their opponents. This allows them to make more optimal plays, thinner value bets and thinner bluffs. It can also open up an online players' eyes to the possibilities for making money by utilizing some of these plays online.

Game Selection

Game selection is very important in poker and this is especially true as the number of players decreases at a table. At a full table if there is one really bad player the benefits of his lack of skill will be shared by the entire table. At the other end of the spectrum is heads up play where 100% of the equity an opponents gives up will go straight to you.

Additionally, at a full table it will take more time to reap the benefits of playing against a bad player because everyone plays so many fewer hands with more people at a table, and thus there are fewer occasions when you and the bad player are in the pot together where you are earning money because of his mistakes. Of course, the opposite is true and if you are the inferior player in a heads-up match you will lose your money faster. Therefore, especially in heads-up play, it is important to find the good tables and to leave the bad ones alone.

Just how important this is, is obscured by the idea of win rates. Take the amount of money won and divide by hours played and this is your hourly rate. It is helpful information but it is an aggregate of other information, and thus misrepresents what really happened. It can be used productively, but must also be used carefully. This is because the notion of "hourly rate" makes it look like for every hour played the expected value was the stated amount, and that for any given hour in the future the same expected win rate holds true.

However many factors affect expected win rate in different situations. Maybe your opponents were worse than average in certain games, or maybe your opponents were a lot better than normal. Maybe your opponents were average but you were playing particularly good poker or maybe they went on tilt for fifteen minutes. All of these factors are very important to consider since when playing poker vague thinking is a killer. In the middle of a session, being mindful of them will pay dividends. Constantly and consciously evaluate the game you are in. Ask yourself questions such as "Does this opponent have a tendency to go on tilt?" and "Am I a lot better than him or just a little better?". And then perhaps say "If I'm just a little better maybe it's not worth it to play him because I can simply choose a different game versus an even worse opponent" and so on.

Part of game selection cannot be controlled. For instance, without sitting in a game it's often hard to tell whether someone is playing very poorly, whether someone is tilting, or whether a new player you are unfamiliar with is bad or good. Also as far as tilt goes, in a HU match people generally don't start out on tilt. It takes some time until something happens that will set them off and you can't control that – it just happens and you have to wait for it. What can be controlled is what level of effort you put into evaluating how good the game is for you. The more effort you put in the sooner you can decide whether it's a good game or bad game, and by what degree – and then you can make good game selection decisions and do any number of things, such as change tables, play a longer session than normal or leave immediately. These are all opportunities to exercise good game selection, and consequently increase your win rate.

Putting numbers on this will illustrate just how important good game selection is. Playing a table of $5/$10 NLHE might yield Player X $200 an hour on average. However if he has a tilt problem and every now and then tilts in a very serious way for 10 minutes, during that time period he might average -$2,500 an hour. Also, sometimes he plays heads up but only versus players he knows are bad and here he averages $1,000 an hour.

These numbers are made up but they are also quite plausible, since there is a huge range in what is possible for individual win rates which will average out over time to an hourly rate. The key is to make the average turn out as high as possible by acting on the information seen in the individual win rates. What Player X needs to do is stop tilting, but if he can't he needs to exercise good game selection and just leave a table when he is tilting. Note that -$2,500 an hour comes out to -$416.66 for every 10 minutes. If normally he tilts for 10 minutes, maybe he could raise his level of discipline and awareness so that after 5 minutes he realizes what is happening, and at that point exercise good game selection and leaves. That would save him $208.33 which is a full hour of work for him according to his hourly rate. By doing that little thing he saves himself a full hour of work in the future – that is how important game selection is.

Another option suggested by this information is that player X only play HU matches since he earns so much more in that compared to his normal $200 an hour yield. Unless the HU games are both rare and also he really needs all the money he can get his hands on and/or he enjoys playing his normal game that earns $200 an hour, it makes a lot more sense to just wait for HU matches, since he only needs to play one hour of a good HU match to make what would have taken five hours of the normal game.

Another advantage of good game selection is that it reduces the importance of variance. Say Player X plays someone at a win rate of $1,000 an hour, someone else at a win rate of $0 an hour, and a third player at a win rate of -$1,000 an hour. During five hours of play vs. each of those people Player X gets very unlucky and losses $4,000 in expected value vs. the first player which means $5,000 − $4,000 = $1,000 won. Versus the second player it is $0 won -$4,000 = $4,000 lost. And finally vs. the last opponent Player X lost $5,000 in expected value and then another $4,000 which comes out to a $9,000 loss.

Note that the variance was the same in each of these matches. However, even when Player X got unlucky versus the bad player he still won overall. To the outside spectator this can be confusing. If Player X only plays bad people he will always win (unless he either gets especially unlucky, or as the time period gets shortened it becomes more and more likely for Player X to lose). To the outsider it appears as if Player X is really lucky, but that's not the case – he experiences the same variance as everyone but is so much better than his opponent that he still manages to win even when unlucky. Note also how being a really good player and exercising good game selection are effectively the same thing, since skill in poker is always relative.

Versus the better player the session was a disaster. Even if the variance had been completely reversed so it was in Player X's favor and he won $4,000 more than he should have he still would lose $5,000 according to his win rate and come out down $1,000. What Player X should have done is play for as many hours as possible versus the bad player, and quit versus the other two players as soon as he had played enough hands to evaluate them as skilled opponents.

This point about relativity in poker is very important and the only thing that matters is how someone matches up against you. A player could be good but relative to you (since you are a very good player) you would consider them bad. Similarly, in the many hand examples that follow in this book a constant refrain when describing the opponent is "he is bad" or "he is easy to read." These opponents really aren't that bad, and if they simply played against a different opponent at the same stakes they could be favorites, or if they moved down in stakes then once again they would probably do fine. They are not bad opponents per se – simply worse than me. Most of the hands are examples of good game selection by me and bad game selection by my opponents, and for the most part my opponents suffer for it.

Game selection is also relevant in terms of your general poker schedule. Some people like to log a certain amount of time per day and quit. Others will play and then quit to lock up a win, or if they lose keep playing until they get even. Others will do the opposite and if they are winning keep playing and if losing stop. The right course of action is certainly to play longer when you are winning and quit earlier when you are losing rather than set specific times for yourself to play, which makes you inflexible. If you are winning this increases the chances that the game is good so you should keep playing. If you are losing it increases the chances that the game is bad and you should quit. Similarly, if you are winning it probably means you are playing good and now your confidence is especially high so you should keep playing, and if you are losing you are probably playing bad and now your confidence is low so you should quit.

Bankroll management

During your progression as a poker player there will be times when you have to make the decision whether or not to move up in stakes. To do this you have to be in tune with yourself and be aware of your goals in poker. Be introspective and ask yourself important questions like "Am I committed to putting a lot of time into poker for the long haul or not?" or "Do I want to play for a living?".

The significance of these questions is that moving up in stakes is normally an investment. It is rare that when someone moves up in stakes they are immediate winners – the more likely outcome is an initial struggle to make it there. It will take significant investments of time to learn to adjust and improve to win at the new stakes. However that investment will pay off in the long run because moving up in stakes is a way to increase your win rate, and in poker win rates can improve with huge leaps or even exponentially. The question is are you going to put in the time and thinking required?

You may also ask yourself, "Do I have a family to support?" One of the most common ways for a person to tilt is when they are playing for money that is important to them. If you live off your money, or need it to support a family then the money you are playing with and money you are playing to win becomes even more important to you. Losing will cause a lot of stress which is bad for living a healthy life, but additionally for playing good poker.

Then you may ask "Do I tilt easily?". The previous paragraph gave reasons why a person might tilt easily but – even ignoring that – a person might tilt more easily than most people just because it is in their personality. Be honest with yourself. If you have better mental discipline than most then you can move up in stakes faster, and if you lose it's not as bad as for most people because you won't compound the problem by going on tilt and losing even more. If however you do tilt relatively easily, you have to be more conservative with bankroll management and moving up in stakes.

Finally you must ask "How good am I?". This is a straightforward question and, obviously, the better a player is, the less variance will affect them because they could be so good relative to their opponents that they win even when experiencing negative variance. Thus if variance isn't as much of an issue, a smaller bankroll is needed to sustain losses due to variance and the better a player is, the less money they need to try moving up in stakes.

Keep in mind that when you move up it will take some time to adjust to new and better players. You might want to try playing a couple of tables at your current level and adding one table of a higher stakes game. That way, if you lose at the higher stakes game while you are adjusting, you will be bankrolling your losses by playing two tables of the game you are comfortable with. Think of this adjustment period as an investment and soon you will learn and adjust to be able to play higher stakes successfully and make more money.

An additional advantage to moving up in stakes is that you are forced to refocus your game and improve your play. For example, when I started out in poker I moved up in stakes very aggressively. If I had ten buy ins to my name I considered that enough to play at a given level. Or if for some reason I didn't have a lot of money online and had to start out at stakes extra low for me I'd give the stakes a go at five buy-ins (although granted I did have more money in the bank) because my skill advantage was so huge over lower stakes players. The reason this worked for me is I had good mental discipline – I had no expenses or responsibilities and I was very committed to the long term and ramping up my win rate as high as I could. So even if I lost money I could justify it to myself as an investment in the future and not be bothered too much. Also I had a lot of flexible free time so if I jumped up in stakes and lost I was able to play more hours than normal at lower stakes to win it back and then give the higher stakes another go.

Now five years later things are very different for me. A lot of my money is invested and poker is a part time job. I am not interested in making it the centerpoint of my life, and am not interested in studying the game as intensely as is needed to improve and move up in stakes further. Necessarily because of poker's place in my life I play worse now than I used to – either you are moving up the ladder or down, it's hard to stay in the same place. Now although I have much more money to my name then I used to I actually play lower stakes.

Multitabling

It's worth talking a little about how to approach online poker and the ability that comes with it to play as many tables as you like. There are a couple of different issues here. One is that playing more than one table is good because then you play more hands overall, face more decisions and thus gain experience faster. On the other hand if you play too many tables this advantage is negated because the action will move too fast for you to think about hands and actually learn from them.

It's best to start out with one or two tables when new to online poker to just become accustomed with the game. With more experience it's important to add more tables not only for the simple reason that it creates a higher win rate but also for the reasons mentioned above. However even if your highest win rate might be achieved with 10 tables, you should reject this option. In the short run it might make you more money, but the fact is it will slow your learning down and so you will improve less and move up in stakes more slowly. The key is to find a good balance – but if in doubt the focus should always be on learning and getting better for the future.

Chapter Four

Poker Math

Expected Value (EV)

In poker, expected value (EV) is a frequently used term. It means how much you are expected to win in a certain situation on average. An EV calculation is simply an actual math calculation to figure out more exactly what someone's $EV (their real money expectation) is in a pot. EV calculations are good practice, and are well worth carrying out to increase your learning. However they are important for a better reason – they are a mathematical way of writing out what is really happening in every hand of poker, whether it's thought about in these terms or not.

Basic probability

Let' start with the some basic math – for example the odds of hitting a flush draw. There are 52 cards in a deck, five of which are visible after the flop – the three on the board and the two in your hand. There are either two flush cards in your hand and two on the board, or three on the board and one on your hand. That means there are 9 flush cards left in the deck out of 47 unseen cards. The odds of one coming on the turn is simply 9/47. The odds of two flush cards coming consecutively is 9/47 * 8/46. The odds of one flush card coming and one non flush card is 9/47 * 38/46. The odds of no flush card coming twice is 38/47 * 37/46.

We can't do such multiplications in real time so a good way to calculate the odds if we are considering a "two street scenario" is to estimate based on a few facts. With six outs and two cards to come (e.g. a two overcard draw) the odds of it of hitting are slightly worse than 3-1, i.e. it will happen 1/4 times. The odds of a nine-outer coming (e.g. a flush draw) is a little better than 2-1 or 1/3 times. And the odds of a 12-outer hitting (e.g. a flush draw and overcard) is almost even money. These numbers can be used as a point of reference, so if the number of outs is somewhere near these numbers, the probability can be estimated by raising or lowering one of these memorized examples as needed.

When counting outs, runner-runner flush draws and straight draws are also worth considering. Say the board is 5♥-6♥-9♦ and I have A♥-2♣, the odds that the flush comes are 10/47 * 9/46 = 0.042, which adds about 4% to the chances of winning (which is roughly equivalent to an additional out). As will be seen later on, simply picking up the flush draw on the turn (regardless of whether it hits on the river) can be a very powerful weapon, allowing us to bluff and be aggressive. Similarly with a straight, if the board is 3-4-10 and I have K-Qo, I need a jack to come and then either a 9 or an ace so that is 4/47 * 8/46 * 2 = 0.03 or about 3%.

Hand Combinations

Another important basic component of poker math is hand combinations, i.e. how many different ways there are to make up a hand. For example, with A-K the answer is 16 as there are four aces and four kings that can each match up. But if an ace comes on the flop there are now only 12, and so on. Pocket pairs are different since they are two cards of the same rank. If you write out the four different colors for any given card, and draw lines between them representing all the combinations, you will see there are six combinations. How about a suited connector? There are four ways to make any given suited connector (one of each suit).

EV Calculations

Now we have covered some of the basics it is time to attempt a simple EV calculation to see how the math of poker actually works in practice. For example, consider the following:

$$(8/46)(\$350+\$1,000) + (38/46)(-\$350) = -\$54$$

This is a quick way of saying that 8 out of 46 times one event will happen, and when it does we gain $350+$1,000, but when the other event happens (which is 38 out of 46 times) we are expected lose 350 – and then that the overall expected value of this situation is approximately minus $54.

This is a representation of when the opponent goes all in on the turn for $350 more, and the pot is already $1,000 and we have an open-ended straight draw – exactly eight outs that we know are good and no more. One important thing EV calculations show is that poker decisions are close. It might feel like you are making a call for $350 to win a $1,350 pot here, however in actuality the decision is close and whether you call or fold, or win or lose the pot the expected value of the different plays is nowhere near the pot size.

For instance in the above situation, it is bad to call over the long haul as a call will cost us money and the $54 loss is relatively large. Play around with the numbers in the equation and you will see that the pot would need to be $300 bigger to make the call about breakeven and $600 bigger before there is around a $50 expected value gain.

Poker is all about these decisions – not making decisions to win $1,500 pots but making decisions to gain a small amount in expected value.

The idea of an EV calculations is to consider every possible action we can take and figure out which earns us the most expected value. Here the options are to either call or fold. If we fold our expected value is 0 – we can't lose any more money because we aren't risking anymore by putting it in the pot and we also cannot gain any money because we are folding so there is no way to win the pot. The hand ends right there and our expected value is 0. So we can then consider what other options we have and see if they are better than that (i.e. if the expected value is higher than 0). A couple ways to set up the equation are:

$$(x/46)(\$350+\$1,000) + (46-x)/46)(-3\$50)=0$$

Here solving the equation for x, and 46-x (where x is the number of outs we need to have to make our call) will tell us where the break-even point is so if we have that many outs or higher than our expected value is higher than 0 and it's a better play than folding. Another way to set up the equation is to keep the number of outs the same and change the pot size to see what pot size is required for us to make it a profitable call:

$$(8/46)(\$350 + x) + (38/46)(-\$350)=0$$

And one final way to set it up is to change how much the opponent goes all-in for on the river in order to see how much that needs to be for it to become a profitable play:

$$(8/46)(x + \$1{,}000) + (38/46)(-x)=0$$

By taking situations that come up and turning them into EV equations you can learn a lot. By playing around with the numbers and equations it will show what the important factors are in a hand, and how much they need to change one way or the other to make plays profitable or unprofitable. It will show when some plays aren't as important as you thought they were because the EV isn't much above or below 0, and help you decide whether you have made a good or bad decision in the play of an actual hand, so that you will be aware of it in the future.

Putting it all together

Now let's consider a real life example. Say that our opponent raises to $30 and I reraise to $90 with 5-5 and he goes all in for $1,000. This is a classic "way behind or even" situation and it's clear a fold in most situations. Here then is a simple math concept put into words that shows what the math obviously proves. But let's say he would do this only with A-K, K-K, or A-A and consider the EV calculations involved. A-A and K-K are effectively the same if we go all in vs. 5-5 so instead of analyzing them individually we can put the hands into different groups – A-K and the overpair groups. If we think he has A-K 50% of the time and a high pocket pair 50% of the time the EV equation is:

$$(1/2)(1/2(\$1{,}090)-(1/2)(\$910)) + (1/2)((4/5)(-\$910)+$$

$$(1/5)(\$1{,}090)) = -\$210$$

This equation is slightly more complicated than the previous one as it's split up in to two sections. The first side is a representation of what happens the 50% of the time the opponent has A-K, and the second side a representation of when he has A-A or K-K. When he does have A-K vs. our 5-5 we will win roughly 50% of the time, so we win $1,090 and the other 50% of the time we lose so that means we lose $910.

Then on the other side of the equation when the 5-5 goes all in vs. a higher pocket pair we will lose roughly 4/5 of the time, and lose the $910 we put into the pot to call. And the other 1/5 the time we win the $1,090 in the pot. Add all of those together and the result is an expected value of around -$210 which is very significant (although still surprisingly low). The fact that we are risking $910 to win $1,090 makes a little difference, and also the fact that we can outdraw a big pair with the 5-5 helps. Also obviously the fact that half the time we are even money makes a huge difference. So if we compare calling with the 5-5 to our alternative plays, here there is only one more which is folding. The EV of that play is 0, and the EV of calling is -$210, so we save ourselves $210 by exercising discipline and folding.

Now let's make this representation even more accurate. In a real situation he isn't going to have A-A or K-K 1/2 the time and A-K the other half the time. There are more ways to make A-K than there are A-A and K-K combined – there are 16 combinations of A-K and 12 of A-A and K-K in total. So the odds he has A-K will be 16/28 vs. the chances he has A-A or K-K which will be 12/28. So the equation becomes:

$$(16/28)(1/2(\$1{,}090)-(1/2)(\$910)) +$$
$$(12/28)((4/5)(-\$910)+(1/5)(\$1{,}090)) = -\$167$$

So here things start to come back in our favour a little. But now let's say that although he will get A-A and K-K 42% of the time versus the 58% of the time he gets A-K, he might not always play this way with A-A or K-K and always play this way with A-K. An opponent might make this play 7/8 times with A-K because he just wants to get all-in instead of playing post-flop, whereas playing A-A or K-K is easier post-flop because they are already strong hands, so he might want to trap as much as 50% of the time. In this case the equation changes dramatically and now we must weight the hand combinations and then put them in the EV equation:

$$0.5 * 12 = 6 \text{ ways he'll play A-A or K-K this way}$$

$$0.875 * 16 = 14 \text{ ways he'll play A-K this way.}$$

So now there is a 6/20 chance he has A-A or K-K and a 14/20 chance he has A-K which makes the equation:

$$(14/20)(1/2(\$1,090)-(1/2)(\$910)) +$$

$$(6/20)((4/5)(-\$910)+(1/5)(\$1,090)) = -\$90$$

So clearly unless the circumstances change dramatically this will always be a -$EV play. However there are still a lot of factors that can be changed in this or other models. For instance, maybe the opponents could have an underpair and then there will be three groups of hands. Again these would need weighting as its unlikely each group would have a probability of 1/3 – it's probably a 50% chance he has overcards, 10% chance underpair, and 40% overpair.

Or as we have already seen you can change his stack size (and hence his bet size), or add in more hand combinations like Q-Q or J-J in which case an overpair becomes a lot more likely and a call a lot worse. Or maybe he does this with just A-K or A-Q and J-J because he likes to trap with his really big hands, and just goes all-in pre-flop with hands he is afraid to play post-flop. A-K and A-Q are have a total of 32 combinations vs. 6 possibilities for J-J so if he always plays those three hands in exactly this manner it weights heavily towards a call.

This is the underlying math involved in the game and it takes place in every single hand. This is a relatively simple problem to figure out because the opponent has gone all-in, there are no future streets and no more action – just try doing an EV calculation on the flop with middle pair and adding all the possible scenarios such as the possibility you are ahead, behind, the times he bluffs you when you are ahead, the times he gives you a free card when you are behind and you have implied odds and so on. It's impossible.

That's why – instead of doing the math everytime – we use concepts to guide us through these situations. For instance if we are either way behind or even money that is an excellent reason to fold. But there are other concepts too that can be important – so here very good pot odds would counter the first concept. It's useful to do the equations yourself, simplified down to the basic concepts involved in a hand, and then to play around with the numbers to see which concepts outweigh others and so on.

Chapter Five

Pre-Flop

Evaluating your opponents

If we sit in a poker game with no prior knowledge of our opponents and are first to act we can only base decisions on our hand strength alone. However the very first action an opponent makes is information that needs to be used in building up a profile. If it's the first hand and he raises his button, I'd assume he's loose and aggressive until shown otherwise. If he folds his first button I'd say he is tight. If he raised his first button and then folded his second button I would then reverse my opinion of him to thinking he is tight because it's correct generally to play more than 50% of hands on the button and here he has played tighter than that.

Everything depends on how your opponent plays, including your pre-flop hand selection. The first step is to learn about your opponent and to do that we'll use labels and categories to put people into. But be careful because though helpful, categorizing opponents is inaccurate – every opponent is different and they don't fit into neat tidy categories. Some players are aggressive pre-flop and then immediately slow down, or others might be skilled tough players except for pre-flop they play very poorly. Make your reads on players as detailed and accurate as possible. When evaluating a player the main things to assess are levels of skill, aggression, and tightness.

Playing tight or loose is not inherently bad or good. There are skilled players who win a lot of money by playing tight, and those who win a lot of money by playing loose. There are advantages and disadvantages to both styles. Playing tight will lower the quantity and severity of your swings in poker. But playing tight won't get you as much action as people like to give action to opponents who will gamble, not nits. Playing loose means getting into more tough situations, and those extra situations mean the possibility of making good decisions and making more money, but they can also mean getting outplayed and losing more money. Because poker is a competitive game, being aggressive is advantageous. However it is possible to be a good player and win a lot of money playing more passively than most. And it is possible and not an uncommon problem to play too aggressively.

There are many things to consider when learning about an opponent, although the above ones are the primary factors. You might also consider if when he has a very big stack he become loose and careless or whether he tightens up to protect it. If he loses a pot does he tilt and try to win it back? Or does he refocus his efforts and start playing solid poker? Is he suspicious when you bet or does he take you at your word? If the pot is big on the river and he faces a big bet will he think along the lines of 'I can't call if I don't have the nuts, I don't want to go bust' or if he gets a good hand does he refuse to be pushed off of it? And so on.

Skill level

One way to learn the answer to these questions would be to play HU for a couple of hours. This however is not optimal – poker is a game of adjustments and the faster you adjust the better. Most people adjust quite slowly, so this is a good way to gain a big edge over them. Another way to figure out if a player is good is to play him and then see if you feel like you can beat him. This is what most people do but again it is not optimal. The issue is that emotions are involved here – people have egos and don't like to admit defeat. If he is better than you, it will take a fair amount of damage done to you for him to "prove it" and for your conscious mind to accept the fact.

The way to get a reliable answer on an emotional and tricky question like this is to ask yourself questions – indirect questions that will suggest an answer. Since they are indirect and straightforward questions the answers won't be tainted by your ego. And since they are questions you are asking yourself, it forces you to consciously think about the situation and learn and adjust – a good strategy if your goal is to make money! Questions you might ask include:

"Am I happy when I get into a pot with him?" The reason you should be happy is because you are comfortable and at ease. The opponent isn't making plays that put you out of your comfort zone and put you to tough decisions where what you should do is unclear. The converse to being happy when you enter a pot with him is being afraid and intimidated. The reason you would feel those emotions is because based on your past experience together he has put you to tough decisions and outplayed you, and it is logical to assume this will continue into the future.

"Does it feel like he is always getting good hands?" Though it is possible for people to get a good runs of cards, it is unlikely. Most of the time people don't get lucky and don't get particularly good cards. Thus there is a discrepancy between the cards you think he has been getting and reality, and the discrepancy has to be explained somehow. What is happening is the opponent is tricking you and outplaying you. You cannot satisfactorily hand read against him. If you think he has only been getting good hands that means he hasn't shown you any of his bad hands, which means he is winning pots with his bad hands by bluffing you out of the pot or folding them early on and only incurring small losses.

This gets back to the idea of starting out by simply playing your hand strength and only after you see how your opponent is thinking playing your opponent's hand, which then allows you to bluff.

Math comes into play in poker all the time behind the scenes. But there is more math than just the odds of hitting a flush draw. HU someone can button raise 50% of the time, or maybe even 90% of the time. If he raises the button 90% of the time think of all the possible poker hands that his range consists of – almost everything including Q-4o or J-2o. Here there is no psychology involved, it's straightforward math that you can reraise him pre-flop and he probably cannot call you because the odds are his hand will be quite weak. Or maybe he automatically calls your reraise, then the math says you can auto-bet the flop and most of the time he will have trash that can't call your bet. Or if he is in the habit of continuing on the flop too and is a maniac the first good hand you get you can make a lot of money off of him and you must just be patient.

If he calls your flop bet a lot then he is going to have a weaker range. But if he is very tight pre-flop and then calls your flop bet he probably has a hand every time because he has already filtered out his bad hands pre-flop. Maybe you can't get inside his head, but this math tells you a lot.

If an opponent raises pre-flop and bets the flop and you call, then he often bets the turn then here you can punish him by re-raising. If he does it seldom then he doesn't make a lot of money by bluffing you out on the turn so let him take down the pot and win money from him in other ways, like picking up a lot of smaller pots along the way that he doesn't contest. Bluff when they are weak, and don't bluff when they are strong.

When someone is too loose, loosen up – but not as much as them. When someone is too tight, tighten up – but not as much as them. Saying "play tight when they are loose, and loose when they are tight" makes no sense. It's symmetrical so how can one player gain an edge on advice that is similar to both players? Picture a spectrum with too tight on the left, correct in the middle, and too loose on the right side. If someone is playing too loose then you want to adjust by loosening up and moving to the right a bit, but not as far as them. If someone is too tight you want to tighten up to adjust but not as much as them – just stay closer to the "correct" point than them.

Some of the time the elements of math and psychology behind poker will coincide. For example, say the opponent is playing very LAG so the math says he has nothing, and then psychologically on a given hand you have a feeling that he has nothing and it turns out you're right. In this case you are outplaying your opponent. On the other hand sometimes an opponent will play LAG, so you figure he probably doesn't have a hand and call him down, but he does. Or he is playing TAG so you figure he does have a hand and fold, and he doesn't. In these situations the opponent is confusing and outplaying you. When you notice this happening a lot versus an opponent it means they are better than you, or at least match up well vs. you – so stay away from them!

Example hands

Example 1

$5/$10, five-handed, effective stack sizes are $1,000. Opponent in CO raises to $35, he is a good player. Button folds, and it's to me in the SB with 6-6 and I fold. The value in a low pocket pair is generally hitting a set and building a big pot. The opponent however will not get his stack all-in with me just because he hits a mediocre made hand. So I will have to outplay him and trick him in someway and I'd rather wait to try and do that with position on him, and a hand that will hit the flop more often then the 8-1 of hitting a set. 6-6 also has showdown value but vs. a skilled opponent, he will not let me win with a low pocket pair out of position (OOP) if he has king high or ace high, as opposed to a bad player who could very well allow that to happen.

Example 2

$1/$2, six-handed, effective stacks of $200, friend raises to $7 second to act and then the cutoff (CO) makes it $29 to go. Friend has Aces but what are the criteria for deciding whether or not to reraise? Start with the most basic thinking which is what do you have? A good hand, so you want to get money into the pot. Then take it to the second step – what does he have? If he is raising a lot then he has a wide hand range and if he is raising a little then he has a small hand range. A wide hand range means it's likely he has a weakish hand that will not call a reraise and will fold. A small hand range means he has a good hand that will call a reraise and may just push all-in because he will be practically pot committed from calling a reraise. Another consideration is how aggressive the opponent is – if he is aggressive now is a good time to take advantage of that and just call because on the flop he will play aggressive like he normally does and trap himself. The aces will almost certainly remain the best hand on the flop, so that's exactly what you want – him to be putting more money in on the flop. However if he isn't aggressive than just calling pre-flop won't serve to trap him very well because his style of play means he won't trap himself.

Example 3

$25/$50, six-handed, 7-8s UTG,. I raise to $175. This decision is pretty straightforward, the main criteria here is how good I am relative to my opponents. If I am good and want to play pots with them then I will take marginal situations pre-flop and go with them. If they are better than me then I will fold in marginal situations. In this case I am better so raised.

Example 4

$25/$50, K-9o, second to act six-handed. The opponents are very bad, I raise to $175.

Example 5

$25/$50 K-Jo, second to act six-handed. The opponents are skilled, I fold.

Example 6

$25/$50, A-5o HU. The opponent is skilled and tight and opens to $150 on the button, I fold. The next hand I have 9-5o on the button and raise to $150 to take advantage of his tightness. He folds.

Example 7

$25/$50, six-handed, UTG opens to $175, he is slightly bad and loose. I have A-8s next to act. It's tempting to call here and a big factor is how aggressive the players behind you are. If they reraise frequently using their position it's very bad to cold call here, so if that is a possibility it weighs strongly on the side of folding. But if that doesn't happen often then a call is reasonable, though still marginal.

Example 8

$25/$50, six-handed, UTG opens to $175, the CO and button call and I have A-8s in the BB. In an absolute sense all the other players have position on me, i.e. they will all act after me on every street. But what is also important here is relative position. The pre-flop raiser has a good chance of betting the flop again because he was aggressive pre-flop, so there's a decent chance he continues being aggressive. In which case my position is actually better than the CO and button. They will have to respond an UTG flop bet and I get to act after everyone else on the flop. Relative position is an important factor to consider along with absolute position. A-8s is a call here.

Example 9

$10/$25 HU, opponent has $1,300. We haven't played much but he has reraised me a lot so far, and recently he showed down Q-6s after reraising so it is very obvious he is reraising us light now. I raise A-10o on the button and he reraises me. This is normally a bad spot to reraise because of stack sizes since we will be pot committed for a big over-bet of the pot and A-10o is a medium strength hand so he could call with better hands and fold worse ones. Also, he is so bad that it might be better to wait and just grind him down with lower variance post-flop than get it all in pre-flop (even with a small EV edge) and gamble. However, on the other hand he is so bad and his range is so wide that in the final analysis a reraise is a good play. Also he is bad-aggressive and not bad-passive which means he won't be that easy to play against anyway, and he could definitely chip me down if I don't fight back. I reraised him all-in and he called with Q-7s.

Example 10

$10/$25 HU, we both have $2,200. I have Q-Q and raise to $75 on the button and he reraises to $225. Now there is a decision as to whether to reraise him again or to just call and trap. It was close, but there was one deciding factor that made the right play clear. He was play-ing straightforward and decently pre-flop. However post-flop he was just a terrible player. So I wanted to make sure we got to post-flop play where he will play badly. As the hand turned out, the flop was 5♦-5♠-4♥ he bets $300 and I called. Again he plays bad so I wanted to let him keep going and give him as much rope as possible so I just called. The turn is the 2♠, he bets $775 and I raised him his last $900 and he called with 6-6.

Example 11

$5/$10, three-handed, opponent opens to $30 in the SB I am in the BB.

He has raised to $30 in the SB a lot. This means his hand usually isn't very good. I have Q-9 and reraise to $90. This is a good spot to reraise for a combination of reasons. First of all, I'm not scared of a four-bet from him because he has opened a lot and I haven't reraised him yet so it looks like I have a hand, and since he has opened a lot he probably doesn't have a hand. And if he does reraise me he probably has a good hand and Q-9o isn't that good of a hand anyway so I'm not losing a lot of value by not seeing a flop. Also if he folds then for metagame reasons it will make my image looser and crazier and next time I reraise him pre-flop he won't know what I have. My style of play is to raise and reraise a lot preflop and hope that tricks my opponent into thinking I have a loose and crazy image, but from there I tighten up a lot and in big pots I am very tight and have a good hand often. This is a good low variance style because in the beginning when the pot is small I am playing "crazy", but when the pot is big and we play around with bigger bets I play conservatively so when I do play a big pot I generally win. And in the beginning when I am playing crazy I am really not giving away a lot, assuming I'm the better player.

Example 12

$25/$50 HU. I limp on the button with 3-5o and he raises me pot to $150 like he has done literally everytime I have limped so I call. The flop is 6♦-9♦-Q♠ and he leads $300 like has done everytime so I pot it to $1,200. Since he has been making this play regularly the odds are good that he doesn't have any piece of the board, and even if he does since he bets everytime it could be something like 6-7 which he can't call me with anyway.

Chapter Six

The Flop

Planning a hand

Having a plan for how to play a hand in poker is a necessity and the time to make this plan is the flop (not pre-flop because there the situation is still too complicated). The plan should be a decision about what pot size will be optimal in the situation and also how to achieve that pot size. There is a big difference between betting all-in yourself for instance, as opposed to check-calling an all-in. Some situations call for the first one, some call for the second one. The more information and considerations taken into account when making a plan, the better the plan will be, and the more money you can expect to make on the hand. More precisely, the more accurate information and relevant considerations are taken into account the better a plan will be.

For example, someone might have the wrong read on an opponent and apply that to a plan – obviously that plan will not fare very well (and if it does, it will be accidental). Or if a person believes one concept is very important in a situation but in fact it may not be relevant, then again the plan is a poor one. The only way to become good at poker is to make a lot of plans and study, and then you will improve and your plans will be more precise.

In poker it is absolutely key to think in specific terms and not allow vague and hazy thinking to get in the way. When considering a play, think about what specific things it will accomplish. And when we say "accomplish," our goal is to win money. So calling because we are curious to see the opponent's hand does accomplish something – it satisfies our curiosity, but it does not satisfy our main goal which is to win money.

In this chapter we'll start introducing the considerations that need to be taken into account when making a plan. Then we'll make plans for hands based off those considerations. The considerations or reasons that would have a person make a play that we're going to talk about are as follows: gaining value for a hand; making the opponent fold a better hand; preventing a bluff; protecting your hand; pot odds; stack size; position; being aggressive, and betting for information. But note that too many people overvalue protecting your hand, being aggressive, preventing a bluff, and betting for information – those are by far the least important reasons to make a play.

Continuation bets on the flop are also a big leak for a lot of people. This can be corrected in two ways. First, simply play the strength of your hand. If you raise pre-flop and get called and you have a good hand bet again, and if you don't have a good hand check. From there you can mix up your plays for specific reasons. Secondly, avoid hazy thinking. It is the hazy thinking that leads people to think that they need to bet the flop because they want to be an "aggressive", or to "show no weakness." These are such vague reasons for an action that they are not real reasons at all. It's like saying "I bet a lot because I want to win".

Real reasons might be "it's good to be aggressive against this player because he is weak and will fold" (another way of saying "make a better hand fold") or "I don't raise much pre-flop so when I continuation bet the flop it's consistent and credibly represents represent a strong hand" (again, another way of saying "make a better hand fold"), or "it's good to be aggressive because then it gives him a chance to call me with a worst hand" ("value betting"). Remember your goal when playing poker is to make money. It's obvious how making a better hand fold will allow us to win the entire pot, and how that helps us to win money. It's not at all clear how "seizing the initiative" will lead to making money. Being aggressive is not an end in itself – it's a way of playing that in some situations won't work well and in others will work well for specific reasons. The key is to be more specific and to find out for what specific reasons being aggressive works, and then to directly consider those factors.

Doyle Brunson advocates automatically betting the flop after raising pre-flop in Super System, but today when playing heads-up or short-handed this strategy will get you eaten up. Instead, take poker street by street – the mistake a lot of beginners make is committing a lot of their money to a hand on an early street. For instance, a beginner can't check-raise bluff the flop because he'll automatically go all-in on the turn to continue the bluff too often. The expert re-evaluates on the turn – he sees if any good cards have come to continue the bluff and some of the time he'll simply give up. Similarly, a good player will raise pre-flop, and then the flop is another street – he won't automatically bet it, he'll consider his options at that point and maybe bet and maybe not bet.

A very good action that will help us win money is gaining value for a good hand, i.e. getting money into the pot with a good hand versus a worst hand. This doesn't need a lot of explanation but the reason it is such a powerful way to gain value is that when you are betting top pair and the opponent has top pair with a worse kicker (or middle pair) and calls you, he only has three or five outs. He'll rarely outdraw you, and you have a lot of equity in the pot compared to him. Whenever you make a bet and he calls, you gain almost his entire bet in expected value.

Aggression

People usually want to be aggressive to "take control of the hand" or "seize the initiative", however as we have said these are not ends in themselves, just examples of hazy thinking. Taking control of the hand is meaningless, however it's almost synonymous with a couple of legitimate reasons which are "betting now to prevent a bluff later on", and "betting for information". These ideas are more Limit poker ideas than NLHE ones. In NLHE since the bet sizes are not small fractions of the pot but rather close to pot size most of the time, they are significant and can't be thrown around. Betting for information is too expensive, in fact it doesn't really accomplish much except for sometimes making a hand easier to play.

But making a hand easy to play is not the same as making it more profitable. In NLHE instead of betting for information it's better to just check, and then you won't have the information but you also won't have thrown out a sizeable bet, and without the information you'll just have to make an educated guess and come to the best decision you can. Similarly, instead of betting to prevent a bluff, just check. And then if he bets, now you have a decision to make. If you are afraid he's bluffing you a lot then simply start calling him down with weaker hands.

Being aggressive is ok to accomplish certain things – when you are aggressive and betting or raising it could be to gain value or to bluff the opponent. As shown above that gains real money, but just "being aggressive" does not gain anything in itself unless it is used as a tool to gain something. So be specific and figure out what exactly you are trying to gain and figure out what the thing you are trying to gain is worth.

Another important factor to consider is the skill of your opponent – for example whether they will outplay you on the river. If you check the turn and they are a bad player, you can maybe pick off a bluff on the river when the draw misses, and fold when it hits. But if they're better than you, maybe they'll outplay you on the river with a bluff and you will lose the whole pot – so now you might want to bet to protect yourself against getting bluffed later in the hand.

Protecting your hand

The conventional wisdom that says protecting your hands in NLHE is a must is one of the biggest misconceptions out there. NLHE is not like limit hold'em in that regard – you do not bet to protect your hand. In NLHE profits come from value betting against worse hands or by bluffing out better hands. The math shows why this is true. Say the pot is $1,500 and you bet $1,500 into it to protect your top pair from being drawn out on. Maybe they have top pair with a lower kicker, a flush draw or second pair. In case one they have three outs, in case two they have nine outs, and in case three they have five outs, so in all cases their equity is below 1/4 of the pot. So basically you are betting $1,500 to protect 1/4 of the pot, or $375.

Another factor people think is important is betting to protects bluffs in the future. This is related to the idea of betting for information and it's just too expensive to do in NLHE. Instead, if you think the opponent is the type to bluff a lot, just check the flop and then either make a weak call-down or re-bluff raise him. That is how to profit from someone that bluffs a lot – not by stopping him from bluffing with a costly bet, but by spotting it and taking advantage of it by calling him light.

Determining the best line

The main factor in determining what to the best line to take is seeing if when you bet a worst hand will call or if a better hand will fold.. Consider for example if at $5/$10 HU I open on the button to $35 with A-10 and the opponent calls. The flop is 10-7-4. Now the reason I would bet here for the most part is to gain value rather than protect my hand. If he has two overcards like Q-J or Q-K he has six outs, if he has a pair of tens with a worst kicker just three outs, and even if he has 8-7 that has only eight outs.

So we don't gain much value by forcing him to fold but there is value if he'll raise us and we're prepared to call – then a lot of money can go into the pot with us as big favorites. That however isn't really protecting our hand, it's still betting for value. And if he has a pair of tens with a worse kicker he'll certainly put money in and have little chance of outdrawing us and that is where the main value comes from.

Stack sizes will affect the plan you come up with for a hand and what matters is effective stack size, which means the money that can be won or lost based on the smallest stack. We can look at stack sizes in relation to the number of big blinds, and also what percent of went in pre-flop and from this decide what type of hand will be played out post-flop. The general rule is that the bigger the effective stacks are, the more flexibility there is in how a hand is played, and the more money that goes in pre-flop the less concern there is that a player will hit a big hand – if a player puts in 10% of their stack pre-flop, then we're not really afraid of him hitting flushes or two pairs.

Position is a big advantage which you want to make sure you utilize to the fullest extent post-flop. The way to utilize it is by playing as many streets as possible in position to put the disadvantage on the opponent as often as possible. If just one street is played than the opponent has to deal with the disadvantage of being out of position, but just one time. With more streets a person in position gains more information, as they get to see more cards and how the opponent reacts the whole way. The way to play more streets is to play more passively in position. Conversely, if a person is playing out of position, they need to neutralize the disadvantage by trying to end the betting action on a hand as soon as possible by either folding or raising, and in general a person will need to play more aggressive out of position if they enter a pot.

Pot Odds

Pot odds are the odds you are getting to call a bet to win the pot. If the bet is small in relation to the pot, then you are getting good pot odds. In general, on the flop and turn people bet around the pot size, which gives a person 2:1 pot odds. Draws in NLHE are not that strong (almost no draws are going to hit 1/3 times getting one card) so for the most part people don't make those call because of pot odds. Instead NLHE players think more in terms of implied odds – the chances of hitting a hand and winning additional money after making it.

Pot odds are therefore most important on the river where the opponent makes a bet and there is no future action. However pot odds are still relatively not that important even then as making the correct river decision is mainly a matter of hand reading, and then if the decision is close the idea of pot odds can be factored in to sway it one way or the other.

Here is a simple hand to try an equity calculations with. EP min-raises to $100 at $25/50 and LP calls with a short-stack of $3,000. I have A-Qo on the button. The min-raise to me says that he has a mediocre hand that he doesn't want to put a lot of money in with, and doesn't want to build a pot with – he just wants to see a flop cheaply. So I raise to $500, EP folds and LP calls. The flop comes A-J-6 with 3 spades, he checks, I bet $800 and he goes all-in for $1,700 more.

So now there is approximately $1,100 in the pot from pre-flop, then $1,600 more from my bet and his call which makes $2,700, and he raises $1,700 more so I would put up $1,700 to win $4,400 – so 44:17 or almost 5:2. If he has A-J, a set, or a flush then I have very little chance of winning. If he has a pair and a flush draw like K-J with a spade, or maybe 10-10 with a spade that gives him 5 or 2 pair/set outs and 9 flush outs, so 12 on average. 12 outs twice is about even money to win the pot. So the equation is:

$$x(\$4{,}400*0.5 - \$1{,}700*0.5) - (1\text{-}x)(\$1{,}700)=0$$

$$\$1{,}350x - \$1{,}700 + \$1{,}700x = 0$$

$$\$3{,}035x = \$1{,}700$$

$$x = 0.56$$

It's important to understand how this equation works. X is equal to the percent of times A-Q has to be ahead versus a semi-bluff for our equity to be breakeven in the pot when calling. About 50% of the time 10-10 will win so we'll lose the $1,700 we used to call his bet, and the other 50% of the time we win the entire pot of $4,400. (1-x) is all the other times when he does NOT have a semi-bluff – it is the times I'm drawing dead and then I lose the $1,700 call. Note that (1 – x) added to x is equal to 1. i.e. x and (1 – x) account for two different scenarios which together happen 100% of the time. There are two factors battling each other here – the first is that our pot odds are so good, but second is that he has a lot of equity even when he's behind. So from the equation we can see that if our hand is good 56% of the time then calling is a break even proposition. Let's say our hand reading is off and it's good only 30% of the time. Now we can plug those values in and see how much our mistake cost us:

$$0.3(\$4{,}400*0.5 - \$1{,}700*0.5) -(0.7)(\$1{,}700) = -\$788$$

Or let's say it's good 70% of the time then it becomes:

$$0.7(\$4{,}400*0.5 - \$1{,}700*0.5) - (0.3)(\$1{,}700) = \$435$$

Based on the calculations above if we call when we are ahead 70% of the time then we win $435 from our opponents in Expected Value, and if we call when our hand is only good 30% of the time we lose ourselves almost $800 in EV. You can see that by calling or folding we don't make decisions that cost us $1,700 or win us $4,400 – they actually win or lose a small fraction of that depending on how good or bad our hand reading was.

Now let's say he either has A-10o or one of his huge hands then try running it again:

$$x(\$4,400) - (1-x)(\$1,700) = 0$$

$$\$4,400x - \$1,700 + \$1,700x = 0$$

$$\$6,100x = \$1,700$$

$$x = 0.27$$

So if we're either ahead huge or behind huge (and there is no re-drawing) then we only have to be good 27% of the time because our pot odds are so good. Note that this equation is just a long hand way of writing out pot odds which are 4,400:1,700 or 1,700/(4,400+1,700) = 0.27.

Implied Odds

Implied odds are another tool to add the poker arsenal. When a person starts out playing poker they have relatively few "tools" to use – for instance maybe there is just pot-odds, which as seen above do not allow for a lot of flexibility, as based on them alone many hands would have to be folded. As more and more ideas get added into the thinking and planning of a hand, there are more possibilities and more ways to mix it up and either call, raise or bet as opposed to folding or checking and it will be understandable why those plays are profitable.

Implied odds come into play based on how much money you think you can make if you hit that drawing hand on future streets. Your implied odds depend heavily on earlier factors such as hand reading and the style of an opponent. To figure out if you have good implied odds first consider the hand ranges of your opponent and how they will react to the cards coming on the board that hit your hand. Then also consider the style of poker your opponent plays (skilled? aggressive? loose?) and how that will fit into the picture. Implied odds can also be combined with pot odds to find more +EV calling situations.

Here is a straightforward example. Eight-handed $5/10, UTG limps, UTG+1 limps, I limp on the button with K♥-Q♥ and the BB checks. Normally this hand is good for a raise – it's a good hand and we have position, however the reason I didn't this time is because UTG had a stack of just $250, which makes it easy for him to limp-reraise me all-in which is not something I want. The flop comes A♥-3♣-2♥, BB and UTG check, next to act bets pot of $45. Here clearly I do not have pot-odds but if I get paid off if a flush comes then I can call. The turn is a 7♠ and he bets $135 leaving himself with $500. A flush card will come about 1/5 times, and pot odds say I need to win 1/3 times, so I need to make up for that difference somehow to call. The answer is with implied odds, or in other words, the time a flush card comes and he pays me off:

$$0.8(-\$135) + 0.2(\$405 + x) = 0$$

This means that 80% of the time we won't hit the flush and won't win the pot (note this neglects the times when our hand is already good and we can win as is in a showdown, and the times we can bluff him when a flush card doesn't come which are significant factors). And 20% of the time we win the $405 in the pot and then x, where x is the amount of money the opponent will pay of us on average when we hit, which in this case is $135. Note how a turn call is worse than a flop call even though we still have 1/5 chance of hitting the next card and immediate pot odds of 2:1. This is because on straight pot odds we cannot call getting 2:1 on a 4:1 shot to hit, however if he gives us a free turn card then our chance of hitting a flush becomes about 2:1 overall. He will check the turn some of the time (when playing you need to make a mental estimate) so pot odds won't justify the call entirely. However implied odds are better on the flop than the turn because then the math is

$$0.8(-\$45) + 0.2(\$135 + x) = 0$$

It is a lot more likely with two streets of action to go that we get the value of x, which is only $45 here.

Example hands

Example 1

$25/50 HU, I raise on the button to $150 with A-10 and opponent calls. The flop is 4-7-9o. I might check this flop because the opponent is passive and if my ace high is good he will be passive enough to allow me to check it down and win. On the other hand if my hand is K-10 I would be more inclined to bet because king high is much worse than ace high in a showdown. Say my hand is A-7 then I'd ask some questions like "how aggressive is my opponent?". Some opponents will either fold or raise and not call – in that case betting will only serve to protect my hand, it won't fold out better hands or gain value. Here it isn't needed to prevent versus a bluff because my hand is strong enough to call a future bet so it deprives me of a future bluff. If on the other hand the opponent is passive then I'd go for a bet for value and to protect my hand.

Example 2

$25/$50 HU, I raised pre-flop with A-9 and he called. The board was 9-3-4o. Now I'd be more inclined to bet the flop because my hand is better so it is more possible for him to call with a worse hand (gaining value for me).

Example 3

$25/$50 HU, I raised pre-flop with 59, he called and the board is 9-3-4o. Here I'd be a lot more likely to check the flop because it's harder for the opponent to call with a worse hand – for him to have hit a pair means he has top pair with a better kicker, or a pair of threes of fours, but since the three and four are such low cards, it's hard for him to call pre-flop with a three or four in his hand very often.

Example 4

$25/$50 HU, I raise pre-flop with K-5o and he calls. The flop is K-J-8. Here the board is very coordinated, and even though my kicker is bad it's quite possible the opponent hit a second best hand and I can get value with a flop bet. One consideration when you hit a hand and want to gain value is "how aggressive is the opponent"? If he's aggressive I'd rather check to be tricky and try to catch a bluff on the turn and/or river. It also depends on how happy you'd be to call a raise and build a big pot with your hand – if you are happy to do that then there could be huge value in betting and calling him down if he is aggressive and raises.

Example 5

$25/$50 HU, I raise to $150 on the button with 6-9o, opponent calls. The flop is 2-3-6. If my opponent is tight and passive, even though we have top pair there aren't a lot of ways to gain money from this situation because if I check behind he won't bluff, he won't call with a second best hand, and we certainly can't try and make him fold a better hand with a flop bet. So the main considerations are not relevant and we resort to secondary considerations like protecting your hand. Here protecting your hand doesn't gain you much value, but then again neither does checking so it's best just to bet and take the pot down.

Example 6

$5/$10 HU, opponent is loose and bad, effective stack size is $825, I have 10-10. He opens to $30 and because is he loose and bad there is a lot of value to be had in reraising with a hand as good as tens. I reraise to $90 and he calls. The flop is A♠-7♣-8♣. If I check and he bets I will be confused about what to do versus this opponent. That is not enough of a reason alone to bet out, however in this situation the opponent is bad enough that he could call with a worse hand, so my bet serves as a value bet and also protects my hand from getting outdrawn. All those reasons on their own are small, but added together it makes betting the most attractive option here. As the hand turned out, I bet $130 with the aim of achieving all those goals and he called. The turn was J♥ we checked. The river was the 6♦, I check and he bets, and the very fact that he bets makes me think I'm beat, but he only bet $80 into a much bigger pot so based on pot odds I called and he had K-8.

Example 7

$25/$50, effective stacks of $5,000, four-handed. Opponent opens under the gun to $175 and I call in the BB with A-Jo. The flop is

10♦-10♥-K♣, I check and he bets $300. Even though not much has happened, due to the board texture we can already do some hand reading. Would he bet like that if he had a ten in his hand? Most certainly, he could raise with it pre-flop and then he'd definitely bet the flop to build a pot and get value for his strong hand. Would he bet a king like that? This is the crux – he may or he may not. For him to bet the king he needs to be able to put me on worse hands that could call him, and it's hard to do that because of the board – if I hit the board I hit either trip tens of a pair of kings. So maybe he has a pair of kings with a strong kicker and hopes I have a pair of kings with a weaker kicker. However even then he might check the flop, because he isn't going to try and bet the flop, turn and river, so there is no rush to bet. If he wants to get one or two bets from me he can do that on the turn or river more effectively. So it polarizes his hand range such that he probably has either a very strong hand (the trip tens) or a weak hand (not a pair of kings), and strong hands are rare.

Based on that, it's a good spot to raise, and I did so to $1,000. Pot odds are one way of looking at this – we are risking $1,000 to win $650 so he has to fold about 2/3 of the time which I think he will. However implied odds come into play here too because we do have a gutshot draw which will probably give us the best hand. Also there is a chance the ace is an out. Also position is important here so we want to play aggressively to neutralize our disadvantage – so if we're going to make a play for the pot we need to raise and try and end the hand now. Stack sizes are also favorable for this play – if the opponent was short-stacked, it makes it more likely he'll bet the flop with a pair of kings or even a weaker hand he is willing to get all-in with (because he doesn't need to worry about pot control). As it is, when we bet $1,000 if he wants to reraise us he'll have to reraise a lot more, and if he calls he'll have to face the prospect of a big turn bet, so the stack sizes give us power here. In the hand he folded.

Example 8

$5/$10 three way, I raise on the button to $35 with A-Ko, the BB calls and the flop is A-J-4o, he checks and I bet $60. My hand is quite strong, I'm willing to get a lot of money into the pot and even get all the money in here (we have $1,000 each). So a big part of the plan here is how we want the money to go in. The hands that are most likely to put money into the pot here that are worse than us are pairs of aces like A-Q or A-10. Those are the sort of hands from his perspective that are likely to just call when I bet. They don't need to raise because they aren't afraid of getting outdraw (there aren't draws on the board), worst hands won't call the raise and just calling allows me to keep bluffing.

Thus if he raises me he usually has a bluff, two pair or a set (or a pair of aces that he is playing badly). If I bet the flop for $50 and he check-raises to $150 and I call then the turn is a three and he bets out for $350 a fold should be considered. Here his hand range is very different when he does this as opposed to if he check-calls twice and then checks the river to me, where I'd bet as much as I thought could get called because his hand range is very different.

Example 9

$5/10, six-handed, second to act opens to $35, he has $455 and I cover, I am the only one to call with A♥-J♥. The flop comes A♦-4♦-8♠, I check and he bets $50. As far as hand reading goes, there isn't much information to say what he has. He could be bluffing, or betting with any ace or a flush draw. At this point I need to make a decision if I'm happy to get my hand all-in versus his hand, and if so whether raising is the superior play because by calling I allow him to bet the hands he wants on the turn (the hands that beat me), and check the hands that I want money to go all-in against. I'm not too afraid of free cards here because I have top pair and no overcards can come. He could have a flush draw but flush draws don't come along all too often. The main reason for a raise here is to gain value from weaker aces that he might have.

Example 10

$25/$50 HU, opponent has $1,600, he opens to $150 and I call with 8-9o. The flop comes 8♣-8♠-10♦, I check and he bets $150. Here the main concern is how to get in the most money and to gain value for the hand. For him to outdraw me with a straight draw is 4-8 outs and to hit a higher full house is two outs. So those aren't concerns, it's just figuring out how to get the most money in. Based on his flop bet it seemed like he had a pair of tens or some sort of hand so I raised there to gain value from it. He went all in after my raise to $600 with A-10 and lost.

Example 11

$5/$10, it's folded to the SB who limps in, and you check in the BB with Q-8o. The flop comes A-K-5, and he checks. Here there is not much value in betting because a worse hand won't call and a better hand won't fold (with the exception of Q-9, Q-10 and Q-J). So here is the equity calculation of checking. Let's say he has 10-9 80% of the time and the other 20% of the time he checked the flop as a trap with a made hand that will call. And then the 10-9 outdraws us about 1/4 the time:

$$1/5(-\$15) + 4/5(\$20) = \$13$$
$$1/4(0) + (3/4)(\$20) = \$15$$

Here it shows that our EV is good in either case, but it's slightly higher in the case where we don't bother betting the flop. The equation shows we don't gain much value by "taking control" and taking it down immediately. We risk a lot that costs us the few times he trapped us and don't gain much equity because he won't outdraw us very often. However let's change it a little to say that if we check there is a 20% chance he will bluff us:

$$1/4(0) + 1/4(0) + 1/2(\$20) = 10$$

Because of the small but significant chance of him bluffing us that makes it so that betting the flop is marginally better than checking behind. Note how all the decisions are close, but if you keep adding in factors and making the decision more and more precise a better decision is arrived at. This equation will change from player to player – some people trap on the flop a lot which makes checking behind more correct, and some bluff a lot which makes betting more correct to stop them from doing it (although if they do very often then maybe the best way to capitalize is to bluff raise the turn).

Example 12

$25/50 six-handed, I open UTG with K-10o to $175 and am called by the BB. As far as hand reading goes, the BB needs a weaker hand than other positions to call because he already has $50 committed to the pot so he has to call a smaller bet, and also no one else is to act so no one can reraise him out of the pot. Also I raised UTG so he views me as having a strong hand. The flop is 6♥-6♠-Q♥ and he checks. Here is a good spot to bet because of the factors just mentioned and the main goal is to bluff him off a better hand. He folded.

Example 13

$25/50 HU, opponent limps on the button and I check with J-8o. The flop is Q♥-Q♠-9♥, I check and he bets $100. There had been one other hand where he limped pre-flop and bet the flop in a short span of playing so based on that it makes his hand range here wider and weaker than normal. Also even if he does have a made hand like a pair of nines which is a lot more likely than trip queens, I will have outs. So here I check-raise bluffed and he folded.

Example 14

$5/$10 HU, I raise to $30 with 10-9o and the opponent calls. The flop is J♣-5♥-7♦, he checks and I check. The opponent has been playing slightly tight (though not particularly pre-flop) and aggressive. The fact that he plays tight and aggressive, and the fact that the board is coordinated makes a check-raise too likely here for us to try a bluff. We also have outs in the shape of a gutshot draw to the nuts and also some pair outs that might be good, but we might not get the opportunity to hit vs. an aggressive opponent if we be the flop. The turn came a 3♣ and he bet $30 and I folded.

Example 15

$50/$100, opponent limps on the button and I check with 8-5o. The flop comes A-Q-7o, I check and he bets $50. In terms of hand reading I think pre-flop if he had a hand with an ace in it he would raise, so I don't think he has a pair of aces. With a pair of queens or sevens he might bet but he might check to try and trap me for a small bet later on. Also if he does have those hands he might fold to my check-raise, but most likely he has nothing. So I check-raised here to $250 as a bluff and he folded.

Example 16

$5/$10 five-handed, I button raise with J-9o, SB calls and the flop comes A-10-4, then he checks. People like to call with pocket pairs pre-flop to hit a set and then try to get money in. With low connectors people will just call because they are weak hands (especially out of position). With high cards like strong aces they will semi-bluff raise and if they get called try and pair up. So here in this situation there isn't much information to go on but an ace is at the bottom of his hand range and we can definitely have an ace on the button, plus our jack high has no showdown value so this is a good spot to continuation bet.

Example 17

$10/$25 HU, opponent has $500 and I cover. I have J♥-4♦ and raise to $75 on the button, opponent calls. Flop is 2♦-7♠-3♠, he checks and I check. Please note that in general the more I raise pre-flop (and I raise a lot, almost automatically as can be seen by my raise here with J-4o) the more I'll have to check the flop and show discretion. This is because if I raise preflop and then bet the flop everytime I obviously can't have hit the flop everytime and he can take advantage of it easily by bluffing me.

The turn is the 4♠, he checks and it's to me. Here is a perfect example of a time to not try and protect my hand with a bet. If he calls me I have no outs and if he raises me I cannot call. If he beats me I'm beat, and if he raises me it could very well be a semi-bluff but I can't do anything about it because either he has a lot of outs or I'm dead. These reasons are pretty simple and overwhelming but most people let the thought of "look at all those cards that can hurt me, I want to just take the pot down now" make them bet. The problem is the underlying math which makes it a clear fold. Basically, I stand to lose a lot more than I win by attempting to "protect my hand". The math is I either win a medium to small percent of the pot by forcing him to fold a hand that has a medium to small number of outs or I lose the value of the whole pot with my pot sized bet when he simply calls me with better hands, and I lose the same when he raises me with better hands or as a bluff. Also since we have a made hand but checked twice it's a little tricky and maybe we can gain a little value on the river. In the hand the river came the 2♥ and he led out $25. That looks like a wacky bet with something weird like ace high, so I min-raised him to $50 and he called with Q-10.

Example 18

$25/$50 HU, stacks of $5,000, opponent limps on the button and I raise to $160 in the BB with J-J, he calls. The flop is A♦-9♦-3♦. Betting to protect my hand is a bad idea here. Say the opponent has 9♣-10♦, or say he has K♦-2♣, or something even as weak as Q♦-2♣, if I bet he is certainly not folding. And his equity is roughly equal to mine on the flop so I'm not gaining anything. Instead I'm building a pot out of position in a very precarious spot. He could also easily take a hand like that and just bluff me out of the pot which is obviously bad. Betting to make a worse hand call doesn't make sense because his hand range is very narrow for hands like that – he'd need to have 9x with no diamond and even then he might just fold the hand. After betting he will never fold out a better hand, and again consider specifically what hands. The most likely hand that is better than ours is a pair of aces and he wouldn't fold that. We check and the turn is the A♥. Now if he has a diamond in his hand his equity has gone down significantly, and the second ace on the board also makes it less likely that he has one (and also less likely that we have one so he will be tempted to call us down with a weaker hand). Also he checked the flop suggesting that he doesn't have a strong hand so now we can bet for value and to protect our hand.

Chapter Seven

The Turn and River

Sophisticated play

The above poker is basic poker, and applied along with strong mental discipline will yield very solid results. But to play HU and take poker to the next level some new ideas need to be added. They sill revolve around playing well thought-out poker, having a plan, controlling the pot size and getting the money in well. It's just that within that framework some nuances need to be added.

The best players play with precision. If they make a call it's because they think they are best, not because they think they *have to* given their hand strength (they follow their instincts). Some of the times you might have a pretty good hand and call a flop bet, but for some reason you are pretty sure your opponent is going to bet the turn again, and your hand isn't good enough to call that bet. This is known as a weak flop call. It can also happen on the turn. Make a decision about the hand (this is more applicable to the turn call then the flop), make a read about whether you're good or not and act on it. The worst thing to do is get confused, say "damn it" and call, then he bets on the next street like you thought he would and you say "damn it!" (you are quite a bit angrier now) and quickly muck. This is a terrible play and you will lose a lot of money on it.

Conventional wisdom says, "Every time you call the turn with a made hand, and the draw misses on the river you should be calling the opponent's pot sized bet." This is not true. Play precisely – if you now think you are beat you can fold. Sometimes against a good player you call a turn bet, the draw misses and they bet the river, so you don't have any new information and are unsure of how to proceed. This is because they are playing good poker and you can't hand read them. In this case you should make a decision on the turn because you don't gain anything by waiting until the river. Against a bad player, or a player that you can read well you might make calls on the turn and then after gaining more information fold when they bet on the river. These are bad players and you can outplay them. On the turn you think you are ahead, but his river action will tell you otherwise so you call the turn and reserve judgment until you gain more information.

Whatever the pot size, it's very important to play precise poker – don't give anything away and don't play weak. If you're going to play, fight for the pot, mix it up and raise him later on, call him down, or reevaluate your decision and fold. But, do not make sloppy calls and slowly hemorrhage money away to an aggressive player – this is one of the worst poker sins.

Considering future cards

When coming up with a plan, the more future things that could happen that you consider the better the plan. A beginner will start out with the most basic plan, only foreseeing what will happen in the case of a few cards coming. For instance if he has a flush draw he will consider two different cases – when the flush card comes and when it doesn't. However the advanced player will see many different cases. Take for instance this situation. The board is 10♥-9♥-3♠, and the expert has 8-7o. He doesn't just see eight cards that come that hit a straight and eight that doesn't. He sees three cards that give him the nut straight without hitting a flush, a card that gives him the non nut straight and hits the flush and four cards that give him the nut straight one of which hits a flush. He also sees all the flush cards that can come, and also non-flush overcards. So for instance say the opponent bets, and the expert doesn't have the odds to call on straightforward considerations like just how often the straight comes. Maybe he puts the opponent on a pair of tens, and then maybe he can win a big pot if the straight hits, or bluff if the right cards comes (like a flush card or scary overcards).

Another way to consider future cards that can come is not just if they can be used to bluff by you, but if your opponent can use them to bluff you out of the pot. This is more of a consideration the more aggressive and skilled your opponent is. Another consideration is that when you are on the flop and have a big hand most of the time you aren't concerned with cards coming that allow your opponent to outdraw you so much as cards coming that are scary for your opponent and ruin the action.

For example. playing $10/$25 HU if we both have $2,500 and my opponent is playing standard. I raise to $75 with A♥-7♠, he calls, the flop is 10♣-8♠-6♠, he checks and I bet $125 and he calls. If the turn is the K♠ this is a great card to continue the semi-bluff on. He just called the flop and didn't raise so his hand is probably weak. The turn is scary for him and I could have had a good hand already, or I could have hit the king or a flush and maybe even more importantly he knows he will face a hard river decision. If he calls, I most likely have a lot of outs and even if they aren't outs they will be scary cards for him that I can bluff on. That is the power of semi-bluffing – even if he knows I might be semi-bluffing there isn't much he can do about it. Another reason this is a good time to continue with the bluff is that there is no value here in checking behind on the turn, trying to hit the draw and getting more money in on the river. My draws might make me the best hand but isn't strong enough to extract a lot of value on the river so it's not as much of a problem if he check-raises me off the hand.

Now lets consider another hand in even more detail. Suppose we are playing $25/$50 HU, we have $5,000 stacks, I raise on button to $150 with 7-8o and he calls. The flop is 5♥-6♥-Q♦, he checks, I bet $225 and he raises to $600 and I call. The turn is the 10♣ and he bets out pot of $1,500. I'm going to hit a straight 8/46 times, so based on pot odds I cannot call. And since two of those straight cards *also* bring the flush he probably won't pay me off on those because he'll be afraid, so I have implied odds for six of the cards to come. So the math is as follows:

$$38/46(-\$1,500) + 2/46(\$3,000) + 6/46(\$6,000) = -\$326$$

The previous equation is saying 38/46 times a non straight card comes so we lose the $1,500 we call with on the turn, 2/46 times a straight card will come that is also a flush card so the opponent will be scared and not pay us off for a river bet so we just win the $3,000 in the pot on the turn, and finally 6/46 times a non scary straight card will come and we can get paid off for a pot sized bet on river so we win a total of $6,000, and this comes out to an expected value of -$326. This is helpful analysis to do, but doesn't tell the whole story. Consider not just the times straight cards and non-straight cards come but separate the cards into more categories – straight cards, flush cards, and none of the above. Let's say on a flush card the opponent will be scared and we can use the flush cards to steal the pot with a bluff. Then the math is as follows:

$$9/46(\$3,000) + 6/46(\$6,000) + 31/46(-\$1,500) = \$359$$

This means the 9/46 times a flush card will come and the opponent will fold when you bluff the river so you win the $3,000 in the pot on the turn. 6/46 times a non-flush straight card will come and the opponent will pay you off, and 31/46 times the opponent's hand will remain good and we'll be unable to bluff him out so we lose $1,500. Suddenly with this more accurate plan a call can become good. But even this is still a big simplification, as consider that some of the time the opponent will make a big call-down when the flush comes, or that he might even have the flush draw himself. Or even the times that he doesn't pay us off when a non-flush straight card comes, or the times he is bluffing and if we pair up the 8 or 7 in our hand then we win. So the situation might be closer to this:

$$9/46(0.8*\$3,000 + 0.2*-\$4,500) + 6/46(0.8*\$6,000 + 0.2*\$3,000)$$
$$+ 6/46(0.9*-\$1,500 + 0.1*\$3,000) + 25/46(-\$1,500) = \$46$$

This math is an even more accurate model of what is really going on in this situation. It is saying that 9/46 times a flush card will come, and then when that happens, 80% of the time we can successfully bluff the opponent and win the $3,000 pot and 20% of the time he will call us down and then we lose $4,500 (the $1,500 for the turn call and $3,000 for river bluff); 6/46 times we'll hit a non flush straight, and 80% of the time he'll pay us off for the river bet and we win $6,000 but 20% of the time he'll find a fold and we only win $3,000; 6/46 times we pair up the eights or sevens in a non flush, of which 90% of the time this has no relevance and he'll continue betting and we'll lose, or he'll check and have the best hand in a showdown, but maybe a small percent of the time say 10% he'll check with a bluff and we can win the pot; and finally when the other 25/46 other cards can come and we'll lose the $1,500.

This all comes out to a profit of $46. It's interesting to see how when we are calling with $1,500 on the turn and planning on $3,000 bets on the river, the edge in the hand came out to be so small. By looking at the math it becomes clear what is important. For instance, it needs to be very clear that the opponent will fold when the flush card comes and we can successfully bluff that card – if not the play losses a lot of value. Note that the better a player is, the more into the future they can see and plan for, and a really good player's plan would include contingencies for even more than what is talked about above. For instance on the turn, a good player would know there are other cards that also bring up interesting situations like non flush aces, jacks or kings which might be good cards to bluff on. Or maybe within the flush cards that could come there will be some that can be bluffed and some that cannot be bluffed.

Ev+ vs. Ev+++

You should always try to find the best line in every situation without settling too easily on a merely mediocre or standard line. There are a few traits to battle here – fear, greed and laziness. Fear comes into play because the line that makes the most amount of money for you might be a tricky line that requires tough decisions on later streets. Or it could be fear that you will look silly and foolish for playing a hand in a different way. Greed comes into play because you could quickly see a line that will make money and want to jump on it right away. This greed will only prevent you from rationally thinking about the hand in progress and actually making even more money. And finally there is simple mental laziness – not thinking about the best line and just playing standard poker – and that costs a lot of money too.

If you make a nice play and win a pot don't be too happy with yourself – analyze the hand and see if you could have played it even better. For example, maybe in a $25/50 live game a quiet kid who is not up to much opens in EP with $125 and I look down and see any two cards and raise to $450. Bet sizes tell a lot, and in this situation it tells me that the kid wants to see a flop cheaply with a mediocre holding. With his $125 bet he's trying to block people up. So I have 5♣-8♣ and raise to $450 expecting to take it down. If he calls I will use my position and superior playing skills to beat him. I reraised pre-flop so there are a lot of high cards like aces, kings or queens I can use to bluff him out. The only difficulty is if he has the hand I am representing, but nonetheless I will use my position to feel him out, figure what he has and bluff him if I can on the scare cards. If I hit my hand is quite disguised. As always this has the benefit of guaranteeing action when I do get a big hand.

So anyway he makes an unexpected call and the flop is K♣-Q♣-8♥. He checks. It's unclear at this point where he's at. If I bet and he raises we're going all-in and probably running some sort of 50/50 situation, or he could fold straight away. So if I bet the two ways the hand could go are that we gamble in a big pot where I don't have a big edge or he folds on the flop because he is weak and I take down the small pot. Note if he is weak and folds to my flop bet my hand is probably good as it is, so there is no need to even bet on the flop and get him out of the pot.

The other option is to play deceptively and check behind on the flop and try and wait until I hit a big hand and get all the money in at that point. So since I have position on him, I check and the turn is the 9♣. He bets out $700, and if I raise he's going to have a hard time putting me on a real hand. Aces bet the flop, and kings and queens that are sets bet the flop too because there are so many cards to come off and slow the action. Plus if my opponent has a draw he might put in a raise and it's best to get the money in on the flop. Also if I bet the flop and he flat called, and the turn comes a flush card and I bet big again it's a lot easier to put me on a flush since most people will semi-bluff the flush draw on the flop.

So here I am in a reraised pot looking at a wonderfully disguised hand and raise to $2,400. It seems like some of my most likely hands are any hand with one club in it that is semi-bluffing (e.g. A♣-Jo or 10-J) or maybe top pair. Sometimes I'll get tricky with K-Jo for instance on that flop because my hand isn't that strong, so weaker hands aren't going to call much unless I add deception by checking. So maybe I have that K-Jo and am raising the turn to freeze him up, value bet vs. any weaker hands he has with a draw and take a free showdown – that's what my medium sized raise was intended to represent anyway. On the other hand I wanted to make my raise big enough to commit him for a big river bet. He calls, the river comes a rag, and he checks. So I bet $4,500, just picking the biggest number I think I can get called. He mulls over it a long time and eventually calls and loses with his set of eights.

Now lets look at another hand. The game is $10/$25 three-handed, I raise with A-Qo on the button to $85 and the BB calls. We have $2,500 each. The flop is A-5-3 and he check-calls a $165 bet. The turn comes a 5, and he checks so I check behind. This is about pot control – I think I am ahead here and I think that there is a good chance I can get more value out of him, but only one bet not two. My hand isn't strong enough (i.e. he can't have a strong enough but worse hand) to call a turn bet and a river bet. The strength of our hands makes it so it's possible to get maybe one bet out of him, and it's more likely I will get that bet on the river not the turn. Betting on the river not the turn is more suspicious to him and also he gets to see my cards immediately – on the turn he has to worry about a future river bet. Also it's a very dry board so getting outdrawn isn't a worry so all those factors make it a perfect situation to check the turn and try and get value on the river.

The river comes a K, and he leads out for $200. What I did here and what I expect most poker players who are vastly inferior to me would do here is be a little upset, maybe a little hopeful that they're still going to win and just quickly call. However that's missing a big opportunity. Let's do some hand reading to see why – firstly, the pre-flop action actually tells us quite a bit. He put money into the pot so he thinks his hand is good. The higher the cards are in a hand, the better the hand is, and the more likely it is the player will play a pot with them. Which means that the most likely card for him to have in his hand is an ace, the second most likely a king, and so on.

His bet size on the river also shows he doesn't have a five in his hand because if he did he would want more value, which means betting bigger or going for a check-raise. A final reason he probably doesn't have a five in his hand is because now there is not just one five on the board but two fives, which means there are now only two fives in the deck for him to have and not three. He clearly is telegraphing a pair of aces, and here an aces up hand isn't a worry – he can't A-K as he would reraise pre-flop. So we are very sure here our hand is either best or more likely tied.

The winning play here is to raise big and make it scary for him and try to make him fold to scoop 100% of the pot, not 50% of the pot with almost no risk to us. In the hand I called and got shown A-10. Maybe he'd call my big scary raise because he's smart and reasoned it out, but maybe he wouldn't. And even if he does it's good for us and our image, making us look scary and unpredictable and letting him know we don't need to have the nuts to raise big.

One note on the metagame there. For me it's good that he thinks I don't need the nuts to raise big because my personal strategy in poker (although this can change depending on the opponent) is to normally have a big hand when I raise big, so I want him to think the opposite of me. However there is nothing inherently good about that – for some people maybe they would want to cultivate the opposite image of being tight and only raising big when they have a good hand and then play the opposite and take advantage of that by bluffing.

It depends on what style you like to play, and it also depends on the natural style of the opponent. For instance if the opponent is naturally a loose crazy player then he already makes the error of playing too many big pots. It would be a lot of work to make this player reverse his tendencies completely and try and make money of off him by developing a tight image and bluffing him. It makes a lot more sense to take advantage of his natural weakness and develop a wild bluffing image, and then in reality play tight and solid and make money when he calls and you have a good hand. In poker it's important not just to find a play that makes us money. The key is always to compare all the different options and find which has the highest EV. So even if one play has an EV of $200, don't immediately make that play – consider if other option yield a higher $EV.

Brunson also said that the flop is where he makes all his decisions on the hand but this is also not an optimal strategy. The basic idea is that he was aggressive and that was his system. This might work sometimes – for instance if playing $50/$100 an opponent raises to $350, I call with 8♦-9♦ and it's HU. The flop is A♦-8♣-4♦, and he leads out $750. Now I could go all-in for $9,000 more and maybe take it down and win the $1,500 in the pot or race it vs. A-K. Or I could call and try to outplay him on the following streets. Against a good player you can't out-play them so be more aggressive, but when playing a bad player where you can play as many streets as you can, get as much information as you can, and give yourself as many chances as you can to out-play them.

So I called, the turn came the 2♥ and he quickly led out for $2,500, which indicates a strong hand for him. So without thinking much about it I figured he probably has a strong ace like A-K. This is a close decision but I'm getting 2:1 pot odds with probably 13 outs from 44 cards and then I also have implied odds. He is a player who calls a lot so I think he'd probably call an all-in with A-K. Remember, just because you have a strong draw doesn't mean you need to raise – a strong draw is still a lot weaker than A-K. Its strength lies in the fact that it is never dominated, whereas A-K can easily be dominated. However, if the opponent calls a lot draws aren't worth much, so wait to hit them and wait for strong made hands.

So I called, the river came the 10♦ and he thought for a second and led out all-in, I called, and he had 44. In retrospect this player is so bad that his instant pot bet on the turn might not even have been A-K – there's a decent chance it's A-A, 8-8, 4-4, A-8, or A-4. Out of position even against a bad opponent it might have been correct to fold here. Since I have position though, things become much harder for him, especially since I've been floating with a lot of hands to steal it later. As it is, the way I played it turned out to be pretty good. Even though he had a set on the turn I had 9/44 outs, or 4:1, I'm getting 2:1 immediate pot odds and he has another $5,500 behind so I'm getting about 4:1 with implied odds which is even money. Then if either of the eights come I can't fold and lose my stack. If a 9 comes and he checks I obviously go all-in, and if he bets all-in it's a tough fold that I may not make in the game but if I had a chance to think it through I probably would since he's a bad player and I might be able to read what he has since when he bets strong he normally has something big.

Bet Sizing

Bet sizes give off information, and you can use the information given off by the size of someone's bet to help read their hand. Say someone min-raises pre-flop to open up the betting. What does their bet size mean? It means they have a hand that they want to see a flop with but it's not good enough to raise a large amount or play a big pot pre-flop with. They don't limp because they don't want to have to call a raise behind them. Basically what it means is they are trying to see the flop as cheaply as possible. This can be a good spot to auto-raise with any two cards (this can't be done every time though or your opponent will know something is up and play back at you). It takes time and experience and it's a continual process of refining how to change gears and how often these plays can be done.

For example consider a hand of HU $2/4 where the opponent raises on the button and I call with 6-7s. The flop is K-Q-6, I check and he checks. The turn is a Qo, I check and he bets $12. If he had a king he would have bet the flop or probably checked the turn again to trap. Or he would bet more on the turn because his king should get him more value than half the pot and more value will probably be obtained by betting full pot or by checking behind to be tricky. If it's a queen he would want to build a big pot so he'd bet more money.

As it is, it looks like he has a mediocre to weak hand or is bluffing. The question is whether to call or raise? A good thinking opponent who has say 9-9 could call a check-raise because they know they induced it by acting weak and it is difficult to put me on a hand. And would a king check/raise the turn like that? A king would probably lead the turn or check-call, since check-raising is a strong line for it.

Of course I'd definitely play a queen like that but trips are hard to come by and it's either trips or a semi-bluff of some sort. However this opponent was weak and if I call then I face the disadvantages of letting him have a chance to outdraw me, or he could be value betting with 7-7 – J-J. A couple of reasons to call here are if the opponent is tough and will call down light or if the opponent will bluff again if I call, but none of those applied here so I raised the pot and he quickly folded

Instincts

It is old advice but good advice that bears repeating – trust your instincts. Do not entirely play on your instincts though, trust them but also logically and consciously think through hands. A lot of the time in a hand you will not have the time or the wherewithal to logically and consciously think through it. Instincts are your subconscious telling you what to do in a given situation given all you've already learned in poker. Try not to get flustered in a hand – calm down, think through the hand as best you can to consciously reason through the best play, balance that with what your instincts tell you to do, and then act. After the poker session is over run through the hands in your head and fully figure out how you should have played them.

For example, playing $25/$50 live at the Bellagio, UTG who is a bad player straddles to $100, I raise in EP to $300 with 8-8, and the next player to act is Lee Marcault who calls and so does UTG (who will almost always call there). This is a good spot to bet the flop every time with nothing (and if your hand is big enough, do the converse – check and trap). The reason is the straddle inflates the pot so it is big and my flop bet will be big. Additionally I'm in EP so I get more credit for a big hand. And finally I'm betting into a 3 way pot which is stronger than a continuation bet into a heads-up pot . Or at least that's what it looks like at first glance. However in actuality I know UTG called pre-flop so he's weak and folding the flop almost all the time. So add these factors together and a flop bet takes it down most of the time. Since that is true, if this situation arose and I had a strong hand on the flop, though the specifics of the flop and my hand would be the deciding factor, I'd strongly consider checking and trapping.

Then the flop was dealt, 7♦-7♥-4♦. With a hand like 8-8 it's not strong enough to induce bluffs here for a few reasons. Lee is a good player so I don't want to be playing with fire and getting into marginal pots out of position vs. him. If I check and he bets there's a good chance he just has me beat with a higher pocket pair, and if he doesn't have me beat now him and UTG can have a lot of overcards to outdraw me. So I bet out $700 into the $975 pot. Lee calls and UTG folds. The turn comes a 7. Now Lee's a good player, so I'm going to tread cautiously and give him respect because he has position and has called two bets of mine already. He is not loose, passive or weak, so if I bet the turn he is not going to call me and then let me win the pot with a marginal hand like 8-8 – he will bluff-raise me, raise me with a better hand, or just fold so a bet doesn't gain much for me here (unless I'm prepared to bet and call a raise). So I check and he checks. The river is an Ace – not a good card for me, obviously. I check and he bets $1,500. My instincts tell me if I call I'm going to be shipping my cards into the muck. I try to reason it through though and come up with rationalizations to call like maybe he is making the bet with a lower pocket pair like 2-2 – 6-6 and trying to use the ace as a scare card to bluff me off my higher pocket pair. Also there are only a few ace high flush draws he could have.

So I call and get shown A♦-10♦. After reasoning it out more fully (again, it's hard to do this during a hand) it is a clear fold. First of all, taking a made weak hand like 2-2 – 6-6 and using the ace on the river to bluff is a fairly advanced play. Most people will just take that free showdown. It means Lee needs to have a really good read on me, namely that I have exactly 88-K-K. Also this brings up another point – my play is totally consistent with A-10 – A-K. With A-10 – A-K I could have bet the flop as a semi-bluff to not let myself get bluffed out, given up on the turn, and then on the river if I hit an ace I'd be pretty sure he's not calling and my only chance is to induce a bluff. So basically he's going to have a harder time representing that pair of aces if there's a decent chance I in fact have the aces myself. Furthermore with 2-2 – 6-6 Lee is actually probably going to be folding on the flop because of all the reasons I listed above about how strong I look. It is true Lee could have a flush draw without an ace so my play is not totally without value but in this case I should have trusted my instincts and not let faulty rationalizations and quick thinking let me get trapped for a $1.5k bet.

Strategic Considerations

Part of my style of play is to check the flop more than most people. This slows the action down and extends it so more streets are played, more cards are shown, and I get to see more of my opponents action. A common response to this advice is "but then can't he just bet into you on the turn with anything?". Of course he can, and if he does that I can adjust by calling the turn weaker than normal, or by bluff-raising it. That is the whole point – I feel confident in my play so I don't need to play it safe and standard on the flop and always bet to make the hand easy to play. I'll make the hand harder to play later on because I'm confident in my abilities. And because there will be harder decisions to make later on in the hand than there would be if I simply bet the flop everytime which will give me more opportunities to outplay my opponent, which is what I want since I fancy myself a better player than him. If he does start outplaying me after I check too much then I will have to adjust and revert to playing a more standard aggressive style of betting the flop more.

When playing heads up the adjustments and strategy you use against your opponent are crucially important. Consciously think about how you are going to make money against your opponent. Is it by being aggressive and pushing him around? Is he going to force you to gamble in marginal spots or can you wait for big hands? Here is an example of a time where I should have thought more carefully about the correct strategy against a certain player. My opponent at $10/$25 was playing very poorly and like he was on constant tilt. He had $1,300 in front of him and I covered. I limped with 10-7 on the button and he raised to $75, and I called. I didn't raise since he was calling every raise pre-flop and I don't want to put much money in with 10-7 preflop, but I wanted to play the hand in position so I called his raise. The flop is 7-2-2 and he leads with a pot sized bet. There is a very good chance I am ahead against this opponent but the stack sizes are awkward because if I raise and he moves all-in I will have to call but I won't be very happy about my hand. Also if I raise and he has nothing he can fold easily. I should have just called given the stack sizes and the way my opponent had been playing. Since he was playing so bad, it would be almost inevitable that he would go broke. I didn't need to risk my money here, and should have waited for a better spot.

Here is another hand where at $25/$50 my opponent plays okay normally but is on tilt now after losing a lot of money. HU he raises on the button I call with A-8, the flop is 865, I lead out the pot of $300 and he raises to $1,200 (he has a stack of $3,500). I was pretty sure I was ahead but this is the sort of board where I am either way ahead or way behind. Again the main point is that against this opponent I don't need to gamble – I can just wait for a hand and there is no need to give him loose action. This will frustrate him and he'll play worse and worse trying to win his money back fast. Or even if he tightens up for a bit he'll crack eventually (unfortunately in this hand it was me that cracked and I went all-in). The same reasons apply again – if I lose this big pot I could tilt, he can play better or he can leave the game. It's a fold for strategic reasons.

We've said already that it's important to get as much money out of every situation as possible. One more "situation" is a group of many hands versus an opponent. When it becomes clear in what direction this opponent is making a mistake, you'll naturally want to exploit it. For instance say I've raised on every button with any two cards versus weak blinds for a few orbits. The next orbit the same play will still show an expected profit, but the expected value will decrease every time I make this play. By doing it every time it will be easier for them to adjust to my play and fight back at me. So even if an auto-raise is profitable it might make sense to take some of the weaker hands and fold them anyway to show some respect and not get the opponents angry.

Similarly, there is a correct amount of the time to defend the blinds vs. a button raise pre-flop, but most opponents will play incorrectly in one direction or the other. If they are playing too tight you want to keep them predictable and push them further in the incorrect direction they're playing. By raising literally every time you are making your strategy transparent and even the worst opponent will adjust and become looser and start playing more correctly. So it makes sense to slow down in marginally profitable spots with the worst hands pre-flop just to show a little respect and keep the opponent predictable and playing incorrectly. Then as play continues you can slowly bleed the them easily, instead of forcing the situation too soon in a marginal spot.

How often you can exploit the opponent's weakness versus showing them respect is a function of how bad the opponent is, or more specifically how slow they will be to adjust. The worse they are then the more you can take advantage of their bad play without them either noticing or knowing how to adjust, but the better they are the less you can take advantage of their weakness and so more caution needs to be shown in spots that show small expected value.

Metagame

Decisions should not be randomized to be made unpredictable. You should use every piece of information available to weigh the advantages and disadvantages of making a particular play versus a particular play. Then if the result is roughly equal, add in more information and keep adding more information until you can come to a decision. Randomness is not needed to keep your opponent guessing because you can simply outthink your opponent. Instead of making a random play and not knowing how your opponent is going to react your goal should be to make a play and know exactly what your opponent is going to do. Of course all this assumes you are a better player – if you aren't then they will out-think you and in that case maybe more randomness is needed. But in that case if it is HU you should just quit and if it is short-handed you can adjust your play drastically to not enter many pots with him.

Metagame is not as important as many people think. The most important factor is hand reading and if you hand read well and play accordingly, metagame takes care of itself. Players often use metagame as an excuse for playing sub-optimally. For instance bad players often think something like "okay it's the river and I just have a seven high, and I feel like he probably will call my bluff given the action on the hand but it will be embarrassing to lose the pot with seven high. There's always a chance he will fold if I bluff plus it will be awesome for my metagame – down the line he will call me more often when I get real hands!" There is logic behind this line of thinking but at it's core, it's a rationalization of a bad play.

Similarly, a player may bluff a few times by betting big on the river and then bet the river big again. You might think "he's due for a big hand here" or "he was setting this play up with the last few bluffs, he wouldn't bluff again, this time he must have it." This line of thinking is also illogical. In poker if someone has called your river raises seven of the last 12 times then he's more likely than not calling this next one. So don't rationalize your internal desire to bluff all-in because you don't want to give up the hand – he's been calling before and he will likely call this time. Go with your read – if your read says he's calling, don't bluff all-in even if it would make your metagame look nicer and "balance" out your play more.

It is true however that metagame thinking, put into appropriate perspective, will lead you to play better poker. You'll be in some situations with a monster and think "there is no way he can pay me off, there is only one hand I could have here, he is definitely folding" and then he'll fold. So what you need to do is play some weaker hands like that too. For example say someone raises, and someone else reraises. It normally makes no sense here to cold-call with 10-9o. However in this hand you happen to read them as fairly weak, and if you also read that they are smart enough to fold hands that appear to be second best and they understand that normally you only cold call there with aces to trap them then go ahead and call with 10-9o once in a while so you can take it away from them on the flop. You'll almost never need to get this fancy though because most players are bad and actually will get trapped when you cold call with aces there so it is calling with 10-9s that is the bad play.

Another important point is that good players don't make random decisions for metagame purposes. Good players don't mix up their poker game randomly. They don't do it randomly because they are better than their opponents so they don't need to randomize. They get more information than they give away, they can out-read and outplay their opponents, and so instead of flipping a coin on whether or not to call a big bet on the river for metagame reasons a good player will just make a read on the situation – they will think back over the hand and keep adding more information until they can tilt the decision one way or the other. A good player wouldn't make a loose call-down where he knows he will probably lose just so the opponent won't bluff in the future. They will fold in that situation when it is correct to fold, and then if he feels his opponent will bluff more in the future because of it, he will just correctly open up his calling range in the future. In this way he adjusts and out-plays his opponent.

Example hands

Example 1

$10/$25 HU, opponent is playing decent and straightforward. He raises on the button to $75 and I call. The flop is J-J-8 I check and he checks. Turn is a 4, I bet pot $150 and he min-raises to $300. I take my two cards and three-bet to $950. His min-raise on the turn is saying he wants to control the pot size and keep it small, and freeze me up. He is not trying to build the pot as big as he can – he is saying he does not have a jack. With my play I am saying I do have a jack and if he doesn't believe me he doesn't just call the raise of $650 on the turn. He may or may not face a big river bet too. In this particular hand I had a flush draw – the more outs you have in these spots the better.

Example 2

$25/$50 HU, opponent has $2,200 and I cover. He limps on the button, I have K-9o and raise to $150 because he is weak and even though I'm out of position I think I can outplay him post-flop. The flop comes 3♥-4♠-5♦ and because he can float the flop with as weak as ace high and I'll be in tough shape on the turn to do anything about it I checked the flop and he checked behind. The turn is the 5♥, I led $300 and he called. The river is the A♥, and the pot is $900 so I went all in for the over-bet of $1,500. The basis of this play is that my play is consistent and represents a flush and big bets are hard to call.

Example 3

$25/$50 HU, I have two cards and call a min-raise to $100. The flop is 10-2-3 and it is check-check, the turn is a 10, check/check, the river is a 4. He doesn't have a ten because most people would bet it on the flop, and if not they'd bet it on the turn because they have trips and want to build a pot. On the river, I led out $300 into the $200 pot on the basis that I know he doesn't have a ten, so he is weak and my bet is big and very hard to call with a mediocre hand.

Example 4

$10/$25 HU, opponent is straightforward and a little loose. I have K♥-5♥ and raise to $75 and he calls. The flop is 10♠-5♣-4♥, he check-calls a \$125 bet. The turn is the 9♣, check-check. River is J♦ and he checks. I'm pretty sure I have the best hand, and he is straightforward so I bet as much as I thought he'd call. I bet \$65 and he made a silly desperation call with 22. Since he is a straightforward and easy to play against, this small river value bet (where my bet size telegraphs what my hand is) is okay.

Example 5

10/\$20 shorthanded, UTG opens to \$80, I am next to act with A-A . I took my time and thought that I'd been reraising a lot pre-flop and UTG was suspicious and the type to call a reraise pre-flop regardless of raise size. Normally I'd re-raise here to \$240 but against him I now raised to \$280 to extract a little more value, and even more importantly this builds the pot so he'll be more committed to fighting for it post-flop.

Example 6

\$10/\$25 HU, I have 5♣-7♣ and open to \$75 on the button and he calls. The flop is A-8-8 with two clubs, he check-calls my bet of \$125. The turn comes an off-suit two and he checks to me. He is not going to check-raise me so I don't risk too much by semi-bluffing here. When I bet the goal is to maximize the times he folds and to choose the bet size that does that (although technically it is to maximize the times he folds *and* minimize the amount of money we risk – we could bet all in for \$2,200 here but this almost never happens for obvious reasons). The pot is \$400 and in the game I bet the pot of \$400 but this is a mistake – I should have bet \$300. By betting the full pot I am saying I either have a very good hand and want to win a lot of money or I'm saying I have a bluff or semi-bluff and want him to fold – which is what I had. So given my hand ranges and pot odds it is just too unlikely I have an eight for him to fold so he calls with what is probably a pair of aces. Betting \$300 is actually much harder for him to call if he has a pair of Aces with a weak kicker because when I bet

$300 it is a smaller value bet so it means my hand doesn't just have to be very good – it could be just good, in other words it could be an eight or it could be a pair of aces with a strong kicker, and it can still be a semi-bluff or bluff although that does look slightly less likely probable to him now because I bet less. So now in terms of hand ranges I could have an eight, or a pair of Aces with a strong kicker which makes it a lot more likely I have a good hand, and makes it harder for him to call me down weak.

Example 7

$10/$25 five-handed, UTG calls, next to act raises to $110 I call on the button with 10-10 and so does the UTG limper. The flop is 2♥-6♦-J♣ and is checked through. On the turn a 5♥ falls and UTG leads out $230 then the next to act folds. His bet felt kind of odd to me as it wasn't clear what he was representing – normally someone who limps in EP has a pocket pair and wants to hit a set cheap and it's a little hard to put him on a pair of jacks because of his UTG limp. Another factor that makes it suspicious is that me and the pre-flop raiser both checked behind him on the flop, so it appears as if we're weak. His bet size also felt strange and when things feel strange its normally because someone doesn't have a hand. So I called, the river came a 6 and he leads out $650. This continues the weirdness and it's hard to put him on a hand. If he has a jack to be making a value bet he has to think there are worst hands I could have to call him with, and the most likely hand for that is for me to have is a pair of jacks with a worse kicker. So this narrows his hand range down more from a pair of jacks to a pair of jacks with a good kicker like A-J or maybe K-J, so for his bet to make sense he has to have a narrow hand range. I called and he had 7-7.

Example 8

$5/$10 HU, opponent is bad and has $650, I raise to $30 on the button with 3-3 and he reraises to $60, I call. He does this fairly often so it doesn't indicate great strength. The flop is Q♠-9♥-4♣ and he bets out $65. Now given his tendency to play so loose and aggressive and continuation bet here frequently his hand range is weak. Also his bet size is a little small and thus also weak. However our hand is weak too. So the decision as to whether to try and make a play here is close and the deciding factor is strategic. He's a bad player who is going to lose his money to us eventually, so we do not need to play crazy to upset and tilt him because he is already playing bad and will already lose his money. However the reverse can happen, if we lose a pot to him he can change from playing bad to playing good, which a lot of players actually do – they tighten up to protect their wins, and it's also possible they'll get up from the table and leave. Here it's much better to fight the war of attrition – frustrate him, don't give anything away and just wait and slowly wear him down.

Example 9

$25/$50 HU, opponent raises to $150 and I call with Q-4s. The flop is A♥-6♣-6♦, I check and he bets $135. He has been raising pre-flop and continuation betting the flop a lot so I think his hand range is weak and he can have a lot more than an ace. However I also thought that if I check-raised him he might be suspicious and continue with a weak hand. So I just called his bet with the plan of leading out about 4/5 pot into him on any turn. It's essentially the same play as check-raising the flop, but one difference is the turn card could either hit his hand and make him call my bet or it could be a scare card for his hand. From his perspective when he faces a turn bet he will have a hard time not giving me credit for a hand, since he will think "well I bet the flop, and he just cold called me out of position, so he must have some sort of decent hand". So because it's so obvious I should have a hand, this is a time to use that against him and do the opposite. In the hand the turn came the 2♣ I bet out $375 and he folded.

Chapter Eight

Other Concepts and Hand Histories

Value Betting

Here are some examples.

Example 1

$3/6 HU, I raise to $18 on the button with A-9o and my opponent calls. Flop is 7♠-Q♠-5♣, check-check. Turn is 3♥, check-check. River is 9♠ he checks I bet pot. From the play it's hard to put me on a hand. If I have a Q I bet the flop or turn. A flush draw bets the flop or turn, which I did not do so I do not have a flush draw. And since the flush draw hit that is scary for the opponent so it's hard to see me value betting a weak made hand. Also the straight draw 8-6 will usually semi-bluff the flop and turn.

Most people will stop the thinking there but it is right for them to continue since it's quite hard to put me on a hand, but it's also a weird place for me to bluff. This is because when people bluff there should be a range of hands a person can represent. Here, because it's hard to put me on a reasonable hand it's also hard to put me on a bluff because a bluff can't represent a reasonable hand here. So the opponent has to see through the unusual nature of the play and decide what I have. One more piece of the puzzle is that they checked on all three streets so I am pretty sure they have something weak.

The problem arises when we have a tough opponent who sees us making thin value bets and then check-raises the river to combat us – his line is so strange and tricky (checking three times to check-raise the river) then it's time to consider just calling him with a fairly weak holding because it looks like he's bluffing us. Going down this line of thinking is how high stakes HU games become so crazy. It is especially tough if opponents check-raise good hands to us on the river along with bluff check-raises. From his perspective if he actually had a flush checking the river would be a good play. I checked the flop and the turn so I'm weak. He has to hope I hit something that will bet when he checks to me (that wouldn't value raise since the flush hit) but could be strong enough to call a check-raise, or that I bluff the river. It's also a simple matter of pot control for him – with a flush he doesn't want to bet and be called (getting just one bet into the pot), he wants to check-raise and be called (getting two bets into the pot) because a flush is such a strong hand he wants to build the pot. Incidentally, it also would have been a good spot to check-raise the turn with a flush draw. I checked the flop so I probably don't have top pair if I'm betting a lot of turns when he checks twice and I'll have a hard time continuing against a full pot sized check-raise. There is also very little chance I'll three-bet all-in on the turn after checking behind the flop so he doesn't have to worry about not seeing the river card.

Example 2

$1/$2 eight-handed., one limper in EP, hero has A-Q and raises to $9, limper calls. The flop is K♣-10♠-5♥ and villain check-calls a $16 bet. Turn is the 9♣, check-check, river is the J♣. Villain leads for $15. The pot is $50 and the bet is $15 so this will be a bare queen most of the time.- with a flush villain would probably bet more because his hand is strong. Based on our hand reading A-Q certainly looks good here. Maybe you'd ask "what worse hands can call me if I raise with A-Q though?". Well, maybe a bare queen. It's a hard call for someone to make with just a pair but if you are better than your opponents you can think along these lines: "I play poker with opponents worse than me, so if I'm pretty sure I have the opponent beat, I'll go ahead and value raise and since he's a bad player maybe he'll make a mistake and make a bad call."

Beyond that we are not that afraid of a reraise. One reason to be afraid of making a bet or raise is because it opens us up to a bluff-reraise. Here we aren't afraid of a bluff reraise because we are very capable of having that flush. That's what we're representing with our raise. How can he reraise when we could likely have the nuts? It takes a huge amount of courage (and in this case craziness) to three-bet bluff the river. Bluffs happen a lot of the time when you are pretty sure the villain has a weak hand, or are pretty sure the villain does not have the nuts. In this particular case the villain cannot know we don't have the nuts.

Example 3

$25/$50 HU, we have $5,000 each. Opponent is an okay player and is TAG. He raises to $150 on the button, I reraise to $450 with Q-Q and he calls. The flop is 2♠-5♠-8♣, I bet $700 and he calls. The turn is 7♦ and here I made the mistake of checking. The opponent is TAG which means that he is not the type to float with weak hands on the flop just to try and steal it on the turn. He's aggressive so if he has a hand he likes he'll probably just raise the flop, and since he doesn't show that aggression on the flop it's unlikely he'll show it on the turn when I check to him. If I check I shouldn't expect a bet – the only reason to check is if I put him on a mediocre made hand (which I do) and think that my show of turn strength will be too much for him and he'll fold, if I check the turn though it can put doubt into his mind about my hand strength, and also then when I bet the river he also knows that's the last bet he will be facing so it's easier for him to call and see a showdown.

The river comes the A♥, a bad card because it could have hit him, and even if it didn't it's a scare card so he's less likely to call a value bet by me. However it's bad to play poker scared, this card could have hit him, but it probably didn't. Also the opponent knows that I can bluff bet on this card as a scare card. It's also hard to push this particular opponent out of the pot on bluffs, so to take advantage of that we have to value bet aggressively and lightly against him. So despite the Ace it is still a clear value bet. I bet $1,800 and he called with 10-10.

Example 4

$25/$50 five-handed, the SB raises to $150 and I have K♦-4♦ in the BB and call. The flop is A♦-K♠-5♣, opponent bets $300 and I call. The turn is the 4♣ and he check-calls $700. The river is the 3♦, he checks. I have two pair but it's not a two pair with the ace, and there are also four cards to a straight out there. However these things that on the surface are instinctively scary actually don't matter. It's impossible to put my opponent on a two for a straight – the only way of him having it would be if he had A-2 and that is just one hand. Or he could have hit the three – if he has A-3 he hit a better two pair but that is just one hand so that isn't likely either. A lot more likely is that he has A-6, A-7, A-8, A-9, A-10, A-J, or A-Q. It's also hard for him to put me on a two. The river is therefore a standard value bet for as much as you think the opponent will call, which in this case I felt was $2,000. He called with A-10. He might also think the river card makes the board more scary so I can't value bet with my more marginal hands and that I will just bet with my really strong hands (a straight) and everything else will be a bluff.

Example 5

$10/$25 HU, I raise 9-9 to $75 and he calls. Flop is 6♣-3♠-8♠, he checks and I bet $125. Since the cards were lower and it was slightly less likely he hit them, I wanted to compensate and give him the chance of playing with me by betting just a little smaller – $125 instead of $150. If the hand was Q-Q and the board was J-9-3 I would surely bet full pot of $150 because it's more likely he has something and I want to build the pot. Also $125 is fine just because both are equally valid and I like to mix it up. He calls.

The turn is the K♣. Since he called the flop it's impossible to put him on a hand containing a king – he most likely has a pair from the flop, something either connected, or with an ace. Hands like A-3, A-6, 6-7, 7-8, 8-9 or 8-10. It's unlikely he has K-3, K-6 or K-8o. Its possible he has K-8s, possible and less likely he has K-6s and possible but even less likely he has K-3s. Not only is it a little unlikely he'd play those hands to begin with, but the suited pairs that have a king are all suited, narrowing the possibilities significantly. For instance there are only 3 combinations of K-8s he could have but there are 12 combinations of A-8 he could have.

So we have to assume he does not have a king here, which means he has a draw or a pair. The best way to get more money from those hands is to bet the turn. The reason is because it will be hard for him to put us on a hand. Our bet is either saying we are bluffing or hit the king – supposedly any hand weaker than a pair of kings would stop betting because of the "scary overcard." There is no point in checking to trap – if he has something like A-8 he might be scared, but the river card isn't going to help it's only going to scare him more so we have to bet here and hope his suspiciousness gets the best of him.

Example 6

$50/$100 HU, I raise pre-flop with K-Jo and my opponent calls. The flop is J♠-9♠-3♣, he leads out $450 and I call. The turn is the 6♦, which is a good card. There are many cards that make the turn quite complicated – for example a Queen hits all his straight draws, or makes a pairs or two pairs for him sometimes, and an ace might make us lose or at the least get us less action on our strong hand. A ten hits hands like Q-K, 9-10 or J-10, and an eight hits two pairs and gutshots. Basically, when he led out he probably has hands like Q-10, K-10, 8-10 or Q-8. The reason is that these hand have outs, and they are willing to put money into to see a turn. However they are not strong enough to check-call, and check-raising puts in more money than they want to. On the flop K-J could raise but here we call.

The turn is a 6, he checks and we feel great about the hand. So we bet away $1,500. Now on the flop when he bets out and we call our hand looks weak. We could have called with any number of hands, even as light as A-K, A-Q, even A-xo or 7-8, using the strength of our position. Our range is quite wide, so he calls us since our range is so wide his range also becomes quite wide. On the river an off-suit ace comes. Now our ranges are both wide, he called us on the turn suspiciously and then an ace comes on the river. An ace is a perfect bluffing card and also most people check mediocre hands behind on ace high boards. So if we bet again he's going to put us on something like A-J, any sort of two pair, a set, or more likely he's going to be suspicious we missed a draw.

Now on the turn he check-called so he probably has a made hand. We called and didn't raise the flop so we're probably not very strong. Thus, if he bet the turn with a draw he wouldn't have to worry about getting raised off it. The check-call line is of course a typical made hand line and not a draw line because he puts money into the pot on the turn by calling, and he can't play a draw profitably by just calling (most of the time anyway) so as long as he's willing to put money in he might as well bet it. On the river we ask a few questions. What does he have? What does he think we have? Does he call down a lot or does he fold a lot? To answer question one, we don't know what he has but it is clearly fairly weak so probably not A-J. A-9 is a possibility, but just one hand. So we should feel pretty good about K-J! Question two – he thinks we are either very strong or very weak and people get few strong hands in general. Plus we just called the flop and bet when he checked to us, which is not overpowering strength. Question three – he calls a lot. Therefore we should bet and scoop up that value!

Some people will ask how often he calls us. Of course we don't know what he has, and maybe he just has pocket sevens and it's doubtful he'll call us, but right now we're sure we're ahead of him so even if he calls us very infrequently it is still a profitable play. Also, if he check-raises the river a lot then things become trickier and we can't be such heroes with our value bets. For the bet size there is a decision to make too. I could either make it fairly big and close to a pot size bet which makes it look more like I'm bluffing. Or I can just try and price him in on a low bet size which would obviously be a value bet but he might mindlessly call because it's cheap to. The question is whether the opponent hand reads and would be suspicious of a bigger bet and actually have the courage to call it or whether he's a poorer player who is bad enough to get priced in to making a call because the bet is a small size. In this case I bet big and he folded.

Example 7

$5/$10 HU, opponent has $415 and is bad. I have Q-10 and raise to $30 pre-flop and he calls. Flop is 9♥-9♣-10♠ and opponent leads out $60. The decision on what line to take here is basically a pot control decision. Normally with top pair medium strength kicker it is a call on the flop because you don't want to build the pot too big. In this case however we are willing to get all of our money into the pot. The reason is that the opponent leads out on flops enough so our hand is so strong we have to go with it. If he has a better hand than us we lose all our money no matter what. The question is how do we gain more money against draws and worse made hands? The answer is by raising the flop – if he has a made hand then a lot of scare cards can come and also by raising he might think we have a draw. If he has a draw, he has a lot of outs and there are a lot of types of draws he can have so this info doesn't really help us and we can't exploit it that much by calling and waiting for the turn to make a play. So for those reasons we should just raise now. I raised to $190 he called. The turn was a 4♠ and he led out all in for $215 more and I called. He had J-7 and our hand held.

Example 8

$25/$50 HU, opponent is a tilting maniac. He has $7,500 and I cover. I raise with TcTs to $150 and he reraises to $450, but his range is very wide here. It's not any two cards but it's hands as weak as 8-9 or A-5o. This is a very easy three-bet to $1,300 which he automatically calls. The flop is J♦-7♦-9♣, he checks and I check behind. The turn is 6♦. He bets $2,700 on the turn. Give how loose he is pre-flop, and how aggressive he is, he could have me beat but there is just too much of a chance he is semi-bluffing, or even betting with nothing because I checked behind on the flop and he is a maniac. Also we have a few outs even if he's ahead. I raise his last $3,500 and he calls with 8-9 with no diamond.

Bluffing

Bluffing is obviously an important part of poker. Everyone knows this, but many people get in trouble with bluffs. One of the most common problems is that people think once they start a bluff they can't stop and end up bluffing all-in. After you get called on one street most of the time it is wise to give up the bluff. However, if you have a gutshot straight draw and make a bet or a raise you could continue the bluff by planning to bluff certain cards. Like if the board completes a flush draw or straight draw you could represent these big hands. So you can win the hand by making your hand or by bluffing on a scare card. But if a brick hits the turn or river you need to exercise discipline and be willing to give up the hand.

People who either do not have the discipline or skill to make the right decision in tough situations tend to get in a lot of trouble when making bluffs. The reason is that bluffing can put someone in an extra marginal position. Say you bluffed and got called, and then on the next street your hand is losing and you have no outs – that is a tough spot and the key is to realise that the bluff was a poor decision and not compound your error by continuing. If it was the original plan to bluff a second street if called, or to bluff on certain scare cards that come that is one thing, but all too often people bluff again simply out of recklessness.

Another tendency people have which hurts a lot is that if they are about to go to showdown and they have nothing they feel they have to bet. Say a draw of some sort missed on the river. Use your judgment – if you think a bluff will work then bluff. But don't bet just because you have nothing and you feel you have to. Remember to play straightforward. You were drawing, if your draw hit you'd have a big hand and could bet big, but you have absolutely nothing so don't bet big, just give up the pot. That is, unless other reliable information tells you to do otherwise.

Also realise that if someone bets into you on a four-flush board and they are a decent player, they can have more than the nut flush. Think about it mathematically – they have to hold just one card in the deck to have the nut flush so this isn't very likely. They could have a nut flush, but think of all the other hands a good player could bet – he could bet any medium to high flush or maybe he is bluffing. This could be a good spot to raise because they will have trouble calling with less than the nut flush on these scary boards.

Example 1

$10/$25 HU, me and opponent have $2,500 stacks. I raise to $75 on the button and he reraises to $225 which he has been doing a lot so I call with my red pocket eights. The flop is 9♣-7♣-3♣, he bets $375 and I call. He is raising so much pre-flop and continuing to bet so many of the flops that he doesn't need to have a big hand here – I could be ahead or I have the chance to outplay him on later streets. I called instead of raising for a couple of reasons. The first is to play more streets as his action on the turn will give me information about his hand strength and I can either call, bet, raise or fold whereas if I raised on the flop it would be doing so blindly.

However his turn action will tell a lot more about his true strength – note this is true mainly because he is a worse player than me and if he were better than me than his turn action would give away less information and would confuse me so I'd just fold the flop. The second reason is that there are a lot of hands he has that I'm even with in terms of equity like overcards with a flush draw that might go all-in if I raise and force me to fold, whereas on the turn his equity will go down a lot so he will be a lot less likely to semi-bluff me out of the pot.

The turn comes the 4♣, he checks and I check behind. The river is A♥, the pot is $1,200 and he bets out $750. His bet size tells gives me information – mainly what it says is he does not have the ace of clubs. If he had the nut flush here he would bet more money, because if I had a high club I would call for more money so he would be missing value. His bet doesn't look like a bluff because it's a small size so it looks like he wants a call and isn't trying to force me out of the pot. It looks like he has high club that isn't the ace. Based on that I moved all-in. He ran his timer down and called. He had K♣-Q♠. One part of my analysis that is lacking is "what high clubs would he be doing this with"? It's doubtful he is an aggressive enough bettor to make this play with the J♣ or lower, and whether he'd bet or check-call with the queen of clubs is unclear. So his hand range is the K♣ and maybe the Q♣. So even though he doesn't have the ace of clubs his hand is quite strong and my raise isn't big. His bet looks like a value bet but it is possible for him to have a bluff. Also part of the problem is that the opponent is an okay hand reader – if I had the ace of clubs there is a very good chance I would simply go all-in on the flop.

Example 2

$200/$400 HU live against Chau Giang, he is playing weak-tight. I have $50,000 and he covers me. I have Q-Jo, he raises to $1,600 and I call. The flop is 10♣-5♦-2♦ and I lead into him for $2,800 and he calls. This is a good lead because (unlike if I had an ace high in my hand) Q-J has no showdown value at all if it gets checked down. With Q-J I have two overcard outs, plus it's unlikely Chau hit anything here, plus Chau is a weak player. The turn is the 6♠, I check and he checks, then the river is 10♦ and I check. The pot is $9,000, I check, and he bets $5,000.

His bet size indicates he does not have a flush because he would bet bigger with that to gain more value. He called the flop so he had some sort of made hand and then feels his made hand is good enough to go for value on the river so it sure looks like trip tens. Also note that on the turn his hand wasn't good enough to bet for value, but on the river something changed so it was good enough. Two hands that improved were pairs of tens to trip tens and flush draws to flushes, and we've already ruled out the flush possibility so it looks like trip tens. That gives us a lot of power since we know what hand he has. But can I try to bluff him? His hand is strong, what will he think I have if I check-raise?

Leading the flop indicated the board hit me in some way. That could be a flush draw. On the turn my equity with a flush draw and implied odds go down after not hitting and he called my flop indicating he has a hand he liked. A flush draw would probably then check the turn. Would a flush draw then check-raise the river too? Yes, it makes perfect sense. If I hit a flush I would consider what second best hands are going to give me money, and the main one is trip tens. Trip tens are pretty good and will almost certainly bet if checked to so a check-raise is definitely better than leading out. So with a flush I definitely could, and probably would have played it the same (although because I think he's folding versus the line I took – with an actual flush I would change my line to one where I thought he'd call).

He should still call though. In terms of reading my hand he needs to realize a few things in addition to the hand reading we just did. The question is how often do I lead the flop? If I rarely lead then I probably have something pretty good like a set or a flush draw. If I lead frequently then my hand range widens considerably so I can have a lot of nothing hands mixed in with flush draws. I lead out a reasonable amount so when we get to the river my hand range includes my nothing hands along with a flush. And even then he would need to consider if I am both capable and likely to make this play with nothing hands. If not then even though my flop bet doesn't narrow my hand range to a flush then the river check-raise itself would. However I am both capable and likely of doing it here with all my hands.

So I check and he bets half-pot which gives away information. It is a bad play to make a small bet which says "I have a hand I like a little but not a lot" then fold when a good player responds to that weakness. What does it mean when a good player sees a bad player who is weak make a bet like that and then responds with a raise? It shows the good player expects the bad player to fold, so it makes a lot of sense it is a bluff. Chau needed to see the history between us, how he was playing weak and I noticed that and adjusted – then he would have outplayed me and won a big pot.

Example 3

$25/$50 live at Bellagio, opponent has about $17,000 and I cover. He seems to play poker close to correctly, although accidentally – his game is unimaginative and weak. I open UTG for $200 with A♣-Q♥, he calls and three others call behind. The flop is Q♦-7♥-3♣, I check, the opponent bets $400 and the three others fold, I call. The turn is the 9♣, I check he bets $1,200 and I call. The river is the 2♣, I lead out $1,200, he fairly quickly and without a worry raised to $3,000, I push all in for $13,000 more.

On the flop my hand is probably best, but the decision is how best to reap value from the hand. I'm not all that afraid of free cards and by continuing to bet in a five way pot I represent a strong hand (which is what I have) so the opponents will have a hard time calling me with weaker hands. Because of those reasons, I checked for deception and to see what would happen. The player immediately behind me bet $400 into a $1,000 pot – with such a small bet into a multiway pot he must think someone will call or raise him. Because of that, he is not bluffing, and because it is a five-way pot it's doubtful he would be so foolish as to make that bet with a hand as weak as J-J here. Thus his hand is probably a set or top pair. Sets are unlikely by their very nature, plus his bet size which is small doesn't seem like a set because he doesn't seem that concerned with building a big pot.

On the turn his bet size is further evidence against him having a set because once again, he doesn't bet bigger trying to build a pot. He bet $1,200 into a $1,800 pot which is a moderate sized bet, but it would be natural to bet a bit bigger – around $1,500 with a big hand like a set. Note one way to build a pot is to bet small to induce a raise, but given my check-call flop line it's unlikely I'm going to spring to life here and check-raise.

On the river I led out $1,200 to squeeze what value I could out of his top pair since it seemed unlikely he would value bet at that point given that the flush draw hit. He raised to $3,000 and here my mind cracked a bit under the pressure of the situation. I saw his bet size which was a small raise and based on that figured he had a medium strength hand like a set or a low flush, since I had the ace of clubs in my hand so he couldn't have the nuts. Therefore with over 300 BB stacks and a weak opponent I raised all-in as a bluff. He got a sick look on his face. It didn't even look like he was thinking through the hand deciding what to do – it was more like he was just depressed that he didn't have the nuts so couldn't call in such a massive pot. He showed K♣-Q♣ and mucked it.

Now, let's address the mistake I made which could have been very costly. The whole hand I had him read for a top pair, and then changed that opinion on the river. The main reason I changed it on the river was that I saw I could bluff with 250 BB and knew he did not have the nuts. But then I allowed some wishful thinking and put him on the hands he needed to have so I could make the play I wanted to make.

The hand reading that should have taken place is that after the turn he probably has top pair, although there is a smaller chance he could have a set. On the river it doesn't make sense for him to make that raise with a set because he is a weak player. A flush hit so his set could be behind, and more importantly it makes it harder for me to call his raise with a worse hand. He must have a made hand given the action and if it is that top pair we suspected he is definitely not imaginative enough to turn that into a bluff on the river. Somehow he must have hit a flush and the only way he could have given his flop and turn play is by back-dooring a flush with top pair – so Q♣-K♣, Q♣-J♣ and Q♣-10♣ as he'd probably fold worse Q-x of club hands pre-flop. During the hand based on his low bet size I thought he could have a low flush, but that makes no sense with the other information and there is no way for him to reach the river with a low flush. Even though he is a weak player, it seems quite risky to know that he has something like the second absolute nuts and try and push him off that hand.

But he made a huge mistake which he would have known had he spent time hand reading on the river to see if he should call me. How can I get to the river with the nut flush? I check-called the flop, so could I have A♣-7♣, or A♣-K♣? Probably not, as I'd very likely fold them both. A♣-K♣ I might call with the intention of making a play on the turn but on the turn I just check-called again, also an unlikely line. A hand like A♣-Q♣ would make more sense but he has all hands like that blocked because he has the Q♣ and K♣. Perhaps even more important than my flop play is the river play which really shows that I have no nut flush. If I had the nut flush I would bet the full pot to get as much value from it as I could, or I would go for a check-raise. The small $1,200 lead and then three-bet all in is very suspicious. Was it really my plan to bet small so he could raise me, and then trap him for a three-bet all in with the nut flush? Maybe it's a brilliant play by me, but in that case he just has to pay it off.

Example 4

$25/$50 four-handed, opponent opens UTG to $175 and I call, he is a decent thinking player and I call next to act with 10-7s. It is good to call behind with a decent range of hands shorthanded to mess around with the opponent so he doesn't feel free to do whatever he wants. It's annoying for a player to always have to play pots out of position, plus it disguises the times I do have good hands.

The Flop comes A♠-2♠-A♥ and he leads out pot. It's tempting to make a play at this pot given the low probability that he has trips and with the power of our position. However to do that versus a thinking player we have to not only think about his hand range (which we just did and decided he doesn't have a strong hand probably), but also think about the hand range he can put us on – our bluff must be credible. The way I played the hand pre-flop gives information away as if I had an ace with a strong kicker I would re-raise. Hands I would call with are pocket pairs, and suited connectors. Thus he knows my hand range is medium to weak made hands or nothing.

If I raise the flop given that I do not have a strong ace and he knows it, my play is suspicious. A good way to represent a medium strength hand here is to call, because that is how I would play pocket pairs, so to represent a pocket pair I should play it the same way and call. However this is a skilled opponent so on the turn he will know that my hand is probably a pocket pair and that I don't have an ace, and also know that I know he could have an ace. Thus he can continue a bluff into me on the turn. So this is a bad spot to try a bluff here and I have to fold. Compare what happened here to what would have happened versus a weak player. Versus him I could call the flop and then if he has something he will bet turn and if he doesn't he will check-fold, or I could just raise the flop. In either case I can simply worry about what he has – not what he thinks I have – and that would have allowed me a decent chance at the pot.

Example 5

25/$50 five-handed, opponent opens to $175, he has $5k and I cover. I reraise pot with A-Qo and he calls. Opponent is tight and straightforward. The flop is 10♠-10♥-6♣, he check-calls $1,000 and there is

$3,100 in the pot now. The turn is the 4♠ and it goes check-check. The river is the 2♠ and I think there are some hands I can plausibly represent here like A-A – Q-Q, a ten, and a flush so I go ahead and bet $2,700 and he calls me and wins with Q-Q.

The problem here was my reasoning should have started on a more basic level. The first issue at hand in a bluff is figuring out what the enemy has. This opponent is tight, not weak, and that means that for him to call pre-flop and on the flop he has to have a hand he likes. In conclusion, his hand range is strong hands and very strong hands and there are better spots to bluff than this. If I had kept my thinking simple and focused on the right things I would have seen this and not bluffed in a hugely –$EV spot.

Example 6

$25/$50 HU, we both have $5k stacks. Opponent is loose-aggressive, gives too much action and is a fish. I have J-8o and raise my button to $150 and he calls. The flop is 2♥-Q♥-7♠ and we both check. The turn is the 4♠, he bets $300 and he has been leading the turn every time I check behind on the flop for the last few hands so I raised to $1,000. His aggressiveness and loose play had worked successfully against me due to a bad run of cards. It frustrated me and put me on a little tilt and the turn raise was a product of that. This turn raise was forcing the action – here I had no good outs, the opponent is a loose fish and I should have just folded and been patient.

He called the turn bet, and then the river came the A♠. What changed from the flop to the turn? A four came which made a flush draw, and if I had a pair of fours it gave me a set, so the four didn't change a whole lot. I didn't bet the flop, but I raised the turn so it looks like the four could have affected my hand (of course the other possibility is that I was getting tricky with some other hand and the turn didn't affect my hand). The hand I am most consistently representing here is a flush draw. Also the ace came which is just a plain scary card for him. Even though he is a calling station, this card should be so scary to him. It's a close decision but worth continuing my bluff on so I fired out a pot bet, and he thought for a while and folded.

Example 7

$25/$50 three-handed. Button folds, SB limps and I check in the BB. The flop is A-2-4, he checks and I bet $50. This is a good spot for the SB to auto check-raise because it is unlikely I have a pair of aces and it is tough to call a check-raise with less than that on this board.

Example 8

$25/$50 HU, opponent has $10,000 and I cover, he plays well but is a little over-aggressive. He has been reraising me pre-flop a lot and then almost always continuation betting and so far it has worked against me. I raise to $150 on button with 4-4 and he reraises a bit more than pot to $500. I call. The flop is J-8-7o, he quickly leads out $800 like he normally does. Since he makes that play so often his hand range is fairly wide and weak. This is a good board to make a play on him because it's the sort of board where supposedly when I raise I can have a big hand like a straight, two pair or set, or on this board I could have a strong combo-draw like J-10, plus we have deep stacks and he's out of position. That combination makes it hard for him to continue there facing a scary board where my hand is supposedly a strong hand or a hand that has good drawing possibilities. I raised and he folded.

Example 9

$10/$25 HU, opponent is okay and is loose-aggressive. We have $2,500 each. I have K♥-J♥ and open to $75 and he calls. The flop is 10♣-7♦-4♣, he check-calls my bet of $150. I suspect he's weak because normally he raises when he's strong. The turn is 3♣. Now on the one hand I have nothing – I have no good outs because even my overpair outs might not be good, and a couple are tainted (the K♣ and J♣) so that points to not putting more money into the pot. However when I say the opponent has been loose, so far he has played loose on the flop but he hasn't faced many turn bets yet, so if I bet the turn here it should appear strong to him. Also he is weak based on the fact that normally he raises but here he called, and if he's weak then a third club on the board and a big turn bet by me should look scary to him. And even if he thinks he's still good or wants to draw to a mediocre hand he has the problem of being out of position and having to worry about what I will do on the river So it's a good spot to bet, then if he calls I have options on the river depending on what card comes. But as expected he folded on the turn here.

Example 10

$10/$25 five-handed, opponent has $2,850 and I cover. One limper second to act, then I raise to $110 with K♦-10♥, the BB calls and so does the limper. The flop is A♣-7♦-5♥ and they both check to me. I liked betting in this spot because I'm pretty sure the limper has a pocket pair so when I bet it looks like I'm strong but in reality I know I'm really only betting into one opponent. I already know the limper probably has a pocket pair and is probably folding – the BB is the one I'm not sure about. Based on that I continuation bet here the pot of $340, the BB calls and the limper folds.

The turn is the 10♠ and he checks. At this point we know what the opponent has and that gives us all the power. He has a pair of aces. A set or two pair is possible but based on two things he doesn't have that – sets and two pair are statistically harder and more improbable to come by, and also he called the flop and did not raise. Also we are pretty sure his pair of aces does not have a very high kicker because people normally reraise A-K pre-flop. So we know he has a medium strength hand, and he doesn't know what we have.

We could very well be strong given the betting so far, and also given the dry nature of the board, so if he wants to call us down that eliminates a big group of hands from our hand range that would give him a reason to do so. This is also a good time to put into play the concept of us betting a given amount, and that amount really forcing the opponent to make a decision for his whole stack of chips. On the turn the pot is about $1,000 but instead of betting full pot I felt it would make it look more believable that we have a good hand and are trying to milk him so I bet $765. If he calls that then the pot grows to $2,500 and he will be left with $1,800, so he comes close to committing his whole $2,500 stack to the pot when I bet just $765. Also consider that given the nature of his hand – say A-J – he does not have redraw possibilities and he's either ahead or behind. For the standard player it's an easy fold but if he's either a brave and good hand reader or a stupid lunatic then we could be in trouble. In this case he folded.

Example 11

$10/$25 three-handed, opponent has $1,500 and raises to $75 from the SB and I call in the BB with 6-6. The flop is 2♣-8♠-Q♠ and he bets out $150. Here is a time to make a raise based on stack sizes and his hand range. The stack sizes are such that if I raise and he calls he comes quite close to committing himself for his whole stack. So it's a case of me only betting $500 (in the hand I raised to $500), and him not having a decision for $500 but for his whole stack. Secondly he's aggressive so I believe if he had any pair of queens he bets there, and more importantly I think he bets just about all of his pocket pairs. He's a little wily and he might be suspicious when I raise but ultimately if he has a pocket pair the bottom line is he can't do much. He's going to have a hard time calling out of position and he has to assume I have two overcards, a flush draw or a pair of queens. Plus then even if I don't hit my hand I can bluff scare cards. So his other option is to raise, but I raised to $500 so is he really going to put a full $900 more into the pot though with a under pocket pair? It's a tough spot for him and he really can't do much here with a marginal hand but fold.

Example 12

$5/$10 six-handed. A bad player limps, another person who posted a blind checks, the SB limps and I'm in the BB with 9♦-Q♦ and raise to $55. I do this for a few reasons – my hand is a cool looking one, I'm a better player than my opponents, and it's an image play that makes me look kind of wacky so I get more value on my good hands in future. Post-flop I'm under no obligation to continue with a bluff and will only bet if the situation is profitable. Only the EP limper calls. He is a bad player and has $550 which I cover.

The flop is J♣-5♥-10♥ and we both check. The reason I checked is because he is a little wacky and his combination of wackiness and the stack sizes makes it reasonable for him to raise me all-in with a wide enough range of hands that it makes me uncomfortable. The turn is a 3♣. Since he checked behind on the flop his hand isn't that strong, so with a hand that isn't strong he is going to be calling or folding to a bet from me and not raising. Also the turn was a rag so it didn't change his hand strength.

If he calls me in this situation it's really not all that bad as I have a lot of outs and we're building the pot so if I do hit my hand maybe I can win a really big pot. The river is the A♥ so I have nothing. He's a bad loose player and I'm reluctant to bluff him but the A♥ is the scariest card in the deck so I have to take advantage of it here and I bet out the pot and he folds.

Example 13

$10/$25 HU, we both have $2,500, the opponent is okay but pretty straightforward. He raises the button to $75 and I call in the BB with A♠-3♠. The flop is 7♥-Q♣-8♠, check-check. The turn is the 2♦, check-check. The river is the 4♣, I check and he bets $150 which caught me by surprise. He checked the flop and turn so he doesn't have a good hand and then he bets the river which is a rag. What that means is he either has a weak made hand he's trying to value bet or he has a bluff. Given that I check-raise bluff to $600 hoping the size of my bet will scare him more than it's suspiciousness tempts him to call it. In this case he thinks for a bit and folds.

Example 14

$10/$25 HU, I have 9♥-8♥ and call the button's raise to $75. The flop is J♠-3♥-3♣, check-check. Turn is the K♦, check-check. River is the 10♣. Now at this point if I want to bluff it's going to be a little hard because I checked the turn so he won't give me credit for a pair of kings, and if I have lower than a pair of kings then what am I doing value betting?. Thus if I try to bluff he's probably going to call me with just about any made hand. However it looks like he doesn't even have a pair – maybe just an ace high, or some other high card that beats me, so those are the hands we're going to focus on bluffing out here. And to bluff those hands out we don't need to bet the full pot of $150 as that's wasting money.

What we need to decide here is the least amount of money we can bet to make him fold ace high, which I decided was $65 and subsequently bet. In this way, the times that he happens to have a pair and calls us we save the difference between a normal sized pot bet of $150 and $65. Note that the $85 is only saved the times he does call us which might be 50% of the time, so by changing our bet size here our expected value increases by $42.50, which adds up over time.

Semi-bluffing

Example 1

$25/$50 HU against a thinking aggressive opponent, he has $5,000 and I cover. He raises the button and he does that a lot so I fight back with A♦-2♦ and raise to $450 and he calls as he has done a fair amount of the time. The flop is 2♥-3♠-4♥, I check and he bets $650.

He would bet the flop fairly often after I check, and then given that he also raises a lot pre-flop and often calls my reraise too, that makes his hand range quite wide. Since he is playing so loose and aggressive a big made hand can be discounted for the most part (although not entirely). Also since he is so loose the odds of him having a pocket pair are less too, and it can be more weighted in favor of a nothing hand trying to steal the pot. However, even if he does have a pocket pair he will have a hard time calling my all-in raise because it's so big. From his perspective with a medium pocket pair, I could have either have a big hand that has him crushed like an overpair, or two overcards which along with the gutshot draw if I have an Ace have many outs and aren't even that big of an underdog. Because of that, it will be hard for him to call, and hard to call even if he does have a mediocre made hand which is at the higher end of his range. Even if he does call I still have 9 outs and am risking $4,500 to win $1,500. The immediate pot odds say that if I always lose if he calls then my bluff has to work 3/4 times for it to be profitable. But let's say he has 10-10 and he calls, in which case I have 9 outs which has 35% chance of winning. By doing an EV calculation we can see that if he folds 40% of the time it's a break even play and if he folds more I make money. Also this play in particular is good for metagame as it will make him scared and frustrated.

Example 2

$25/$50 five-handed. I raise UTG to $175 and the button calls, he's a little wily and tricky but not good. I have Q-K and the flop is J-J-6, I check and he bets $350. Now it's time to do some hand reading as his bet feels weird here. One possibility is he hit trip jacks because he bet full pot on the flop so he is trying to build a pot now. And with some players they will have trip jacks a lot here, but since this opponent is a little tricky he doesn't need a great hand to float with pre-flop and he is not a nit and will bet more than trips on this flop so it makes trips unlikely just by virtue of the fact that they are hard to hit. If he has a lower pocket pair he would probably bet less because all he needs to do is bet enough to protect his hand – he wouldn't want to bet a lot for value because there is no value there for him. Even if it is a pocket pair I most likely have two overcards to it, and also it will be hard for him to call me, and particularly hard for this player to call me because he respects my game and doesn't want to tangle in big pots. So I check-raised to $1,000 here and he folded.

Example 3

$10/$25 six-handed, 100BB effective stacks. UTG limps, I raise on the button to $110 with A♦-Q♦, the BB calls and so does limper. Flop is 3♥-4♥-7♦ and they both check. Most people continuation bet and bluff too much but this happens to be a good spot and there are a few factors here that make it a good bet here. Because of the way the hand developed we happen to be able to represent more strength here than is usual and that is the key.

Firstly, our bet will be against two opponents and not one so our bet represents strength. Also since there are three people in the pot that put in a full bet pre-flop the pot size is bigger so our natural pot sized bet will be bigger than normal – a full $340. If one of them has a pocket pair maybe they will feel comfortable calling a small bet (because they have a small hand) but not a big bet.

Also one final reason is because the pre-flop action was not raise, call, call. It was limp, raise, call, call which again makes the pot size bigger because my pot sized raise pre-flop came after the limper. And thus it follows that it's tougher for them to continue with pocket pairs because they are weak hands that don't want to face big bets. The crux here is this situation just so happens to allow me to represent greater strength than I normally can in this type of situation. So I should take advantage of that ability to represent strength and bluff the flop, which I did and they both folded.

Example 4

$5/$10 six-handed, UTG limps and I raise next to act with A♣-J♣ to $45, UTG calls and it's heads up. The flop is Q-10-6 and he checks. This is a good spot to take it slow and check behind. First of all by checking we ensure seeing another card and can maybe hit the straight or a pair. Beyond that, maybe he has something and maybe he doesn't. If he doesn't and he has that pocket pair that people like to limp in with from EP then he will check the turn and we can bet and our turn semi-bluff will be equally as effective as if we had semi-bluffed the flop. What we've done effectively is save ourselves money the times he does have hands and the times he tells us that by leading out on the turn. The downside is if he decides to lead into us on the turn and bluff, but since most people don't play good tricky poker this isn't much of a risk. Another downside is if he takes a weak hand he would have folded to a bet on the flop and gets suspicious and calls the turn. That's not really a problem either because if he has a pocket pair, the board is simply too scary and there are too many overcards/draws for him to play around and try calling even if it is on the turn. In the hand I checked the flop. The turn was a 4 and he check folded to my bet.

Example 5

$10/$25 four-handed, I open on button with Q♦-9♥ to $85 and the SB calls. The flop is K♦-5♠-2♦, he checks and because he's in the SB it's more likely he has a pocket pair than two high cards with a king, because with two high cards people are happy to take the pot down immediately pre-flop whereas with a pocket pair they want to call and hit a set and build a big pot. I bet the flop full pot $190 and he called so the pot is $570.

The turn is the 6♦. I had been playing aggressively to make him adjust and call me down lighter so his flop call is weaker than normal. The stack sizes are perfect for this play here, he now has $1,600 left and I covered. On the turn the pot is $570 and I bet $525. The reasoning behind this play is multifaceted – first of all I have outs if he calls (also some implied odds). Secondly, his hand range is wide and fairly weak. And thirdly, the power of my bet is that if he has a marginal hand he isn't just looking at the $525 bet on the turn, he's really looking at committing his full stack of $1,600 if he wants to raise to protect his hand, or he is looking to call a river bet of mine. So I bet $525 and in position have the choice of whether to put that last $1,075 in the pot. One consideration for this hand is how passive or aggressive the opponent is. The more aggressive he is the more likely you should be to check behind and the more passive the more likely you should be to bet. If he is very aggressive and will only raise or fold here than you are devaluing your hand, which has value in the Q♦ for flush outs and even implied odds, into a pure bluff.

Example 6

$10/$25 vs. the same opponent shortly after. I raise J♠-4♠ to $75 and he calls. The flop is 3♠-5♥-6♥ and he checks. A part of me wanted to check because he is aggressive, and it would be bad if I got check-raised on the flop, but on the other hand that is playing right into the his hands – the more passive I play to some extent the more he wins. Let's say he is an aggressive bad player who is just wacky, then in that case I can play passive and just wait for hands and beat him that way. But if he is aggressive and decent which this opponent was, I can't play passive and wait around. Sometimes you just have to play. aggressive and get into tough situations. Note here in this situation how much easier it is to play vs. a passive player (which is the equivalent of saying a bad player). Anyway, I bet and this time he just called me. The turn is the 8♥. I'm not sure what he had but I used the same reasoning as before that he just called the flop so was weak. Then the turn could have helped him but probably not because he was weak, then he checks the turn again and it's very consistent for me to go ahead and bet again and even if he calls I still have outs. Here he folded.

Example 7

$10/$25 seven-handed, I open to $85 and a loose, slightly crazy but decent player calls in the BB. I have Q-10o and the flop is J♠-4♠-7♥, he checks and I check. The turn is 9♥ and he leads out $110. He's a decent player so he doesn't give away a lot of information with his bet – he could have a semi-bluff, a made hand or a big made hand. This is a good spot to semi-bluff raise for a few simple reasons. First of all we have outs to hit a big hand. Secondly if he calls it's not really that bad because as stated we have equity in the pot, and also implied odds to win a big pot. Finally we have position and there are a number of scare cards that can come which we can take advantage of to bluff too like a third heart – our play is perfectly consistent with a heart flush draw, and probably represents that more than anything. We checked the flop so we didn't like our hand then, but then on the turn a 9♥ came and we like our hand now so much we decide to raise – what changed? A heart came supposedly giving us a flush draw. In the hand he folded to the raise.

Example 8

$25/$50 HU, opponent has $1,800 and I cover. I have A♣-7♣ and raise to $150 from the button, he reraises to $390 and I call. The call is slightly marginal, but the opponent isn't the sharpest tool in the shed so that made me want to call. The flop is K♥-5♦-4♠, check-check. The turn is the 6♦ and he leads out $260. This is a perfect spot to semi-bluff, the opponent checked the flop and then bet small on the turn so that makes him look weak. Although to be honest it's unclear since he's a little tricky and he could definitely have a good hand here.

What then makes it a good spot to raise is two things. First of all we have outs – we have the open ended straight draw which gives us a eight outs and also there is a fair chance our ace high is good for another three outs. Beyond that the stack sizes are perfect. Part of the reason not to semi-bluff raise most of the time is the way an opponent can outplay you by reraising your semi-bluff. Here however that is simply not possible for our opponent. A natural pot sized raise for us is about all-in so there is no way for him to counteract the play and its also good for image reasons and getting action later on with bigger hands.

Example 9

$25/$50 HU, opponent raises to $150 and I call with 10♥-9♥. The flop is 3♠-3♣-8♥, I check and he bets $175. This is a good spot to check-raise him – again his bet size is small and weird and he is probably weak. And even if I'm wrong there are backdoor straight and flush draws which are significant as they let me continue a semi-bluff on the turn if I choose to, and if they hit on the river they are such disguised and strong hands the implied odds are massive and I can make a lot of money. There are a full 10 hearts that can come, six non-heart straight cards and also six pairing cards. Here I raised and he folded.

Example 10

$10/$25 HU, I raise on the button with 4♠-7♠ to $75 and my opponent calls. Flop is 5♦-4♦-3♦, check-check. Turn is J♠ and he bets $70. Poker is a complicated game with a lot of things going on so it's important to be able to simplify situations and analyze only the relevant factors. Here the hand turns out to be quite simple and we can ignore things like pot control, putting him on hand ranges and so on, and just look at two things. The first factor is that he made an odd looking small bet so this means he is weak. The second is that we have outs to hit a better hand. That's all it takes – all we need to see here is the weak bet and outs even if he does call us. I raised the pot and he folded.

Trapping

Normally when you have a good hand you bet, and with a weak hand you check. Trapping means taking a hand that is good enough to warrant that bet and checking, which accomplishes a few things. It lets the opponent bluff (although sometimes the best way to "trap" an opponent is to bet to induce a bluff raise), it can also put doubt into the opponent's mind that your hand is strong (if it was strong why wouldn't you just bet it right away which is the standard play?) and with that doubt in his mind, thus create more action on later streets. Finally it allows more cards to come on the board which could make the opponent to put more money into the pot. When you check to let the opponent see another card and you hope he hits a hand, consider what specific worst hand you are hoping your opponent catches. For instance consider the following hand:

Example 1

$5/$10, three limpers, I complete in the small blind with K-Jo. The flop is A-K-K with two clubs. If I check what worst hand am I hoping they hit? There is a flush draw and if they hit that they are beating me. They can't pair up because there is already an ace on the board so their pair would be an under-pair and not a very good hand. The second question is will my check put doubt into their mind so they will give me action later on in the hand? For example would they call me with A-10 on the turn whereas they would have folded it to a flop bet? Another question is, will they attempt a bluff if we try trapping and check to them? In this hand almost certainly not – it's a five way unraised pot so they would have to be quite reckless to try and bluff four opponents out of the pot.

Example 2

$5/$10 five-handed, I have 7-9o and raise on the button, the BB calls. Flop is J♠-9♠-3♣, he checks, and I check. This board is so draw heavy that with either a draw or a made hand, especially since he's out of position, he has to get rid of my positional advantage by raising so on this board texture it is close to a raise/fold situation for him – he can't just call and see what happens. A raise or fold doesn't look that great to my 7-9, so I check, the turn is a J.

He checks, and again this is a good spot to be tricky and check. Remember that in NLHE profits come from making worse hands call you, or making better hands fold – profits do not come from having draws call you. In the first place if he has a draw he is either going to lead the turn or check-raise the turn – it would take a bad and weak player to check-call the turn with a draw (note that check-calling the flop is more reasonable because it is trickier and he has two cards left to hit it). Check-calling a pot sized bet on the turn means putting money in at odds of 2:1 when a flush draw only hits 1/5 times. But say he has a hand like A-Q and we have 7-9, then he has six outs which means by betting and making him fold he losses 6/45, or 13% equity in the pot, so out of $70 that is $9 equity we gain in the pot. Say we bet $50 to protect the pot with the plan of folding to a raise – if he raises he wins $120, so if he ever bluffs or semi-bluff check-raises we are in big trouble. We are trying to push him out and win $9 of EV but it can end up costing $120.

Since I checked the flop he knows I probably don't have a jack, thus he can check-raise bluff me with seeming impunity, semi-bluff check-raise, and this is also a good spot to trap check-raise if he has a jack. It's hard to see what worse hand he can call with, or in other words, how a value bet by me could be successful. The most likely hand to call is a better nine, like K-9 or A-9. So again it's probably a fold/raise situation for him, but less of a fold/raise situation than on the flop. For instance let's say he has a pocket pair lower than nines. If he calls the flop and I have two overcards (and possibly a straight draw or gutshot draw on this board) he has to dodge an outdraw on two streets, and he also has to dodge cards that allow me to bluff him and also dodge my bluff on two separate streets.

However, on the turn the very fact that I checked the flop makes it less likely that I have a made hand. Also he only has to dodge one street of outdraws, raising his equity significantly, and finally he has one last street to dodge bluffs by me. All of these factors make it more possible for him to call the turn instead of raising or folding. So I check for deception, the river comes a seven and he checks. He definitely can't put me on 8T as that would have bet the flop or turn, and it sure seems like a nine or J would have bet earlier in the hand too. So basically a bet by me is suspicious as it's hard to put me on anything, so he might call with a worse hand that he would have folded earlier in the hand, plus there is definitely the chance he can lead out on a bluff on the river. In the hand I bet and he folded.

Example 3

$10/$25 HU vs. a bad player, we both have $3k stacks. He raises to $75 and I have A-10o so I re-raise to $225 for value. I can outplay him post-flop so I'm not afraid of building a big pot out of position with a marginal hand, although in this case A-10o isn't actually marginal because he is raising the button very often and he calls every single reraise. Normally a problem with raising a hand like A-10o here is that the opponent will fold worst hands and call with better ones, but in this case the opponent is auto calling reraises.

The flop is A♥-J♣-3♥ and now I have to decide how to play the hand. Since he is raising his button so often, and because he automatically calls my reraise his hand range is very wide and there is a good chance he has nothing. Also he is aggressive and capable of bluffing so I checked to see if he'd trap himself. He bet $400 and against some opponents you'd have to proceed very cautiously here and even consider folding. But against this opponent after thinking about his bet, his pre-flop tendencies and ability to bluff, I wasn't ecstatic about my hand but checking the flop was my plan to trap – and now here was my chance to trap and I'd follow through with it so I call.

The turn comes the 10♠ and I check again. Now the pot is $1,250 and he bets $800. Before the T came I wasn't thrilled about my hand but was probably going to follow through with the plan and show down, but now I am ecstatic. The only question is whether to go all-in or to call. Again given that he's so loose pre-flop there is a good chance he is doing this with random cards that don't have any outs. Also if he has a flush draw his bets are a little odd because he keeps giving me a chance to check-raise him off his hand so that means there's a good chance it isn't a flush draw

Note that after I call the pot will be almost $3,000 and we only have $1,500 left each. Most people would get excited about their hand and check-raise all-in without thinking about it for a number of reasons. However even though an all-in would be an under-bet compared to the pot size you shouldn't just throw it in there for the hell of it – play precise poker. So I called the turn and the river is a blank, I check and he immediately goes all-in for $1,475 which I call and he mucks 8-6o. Note that given my plan and pot size I have to call any river including the Q♥, otherwise my plan could backfire in a big way.

Example 4

$25/$50 HU, opponent is loose/bad and has a stack of $2k, I cover. I limp on button with 5-7s and he raises to $150 which he likes to do frequently. The flop is Q-Q-5 and he leads out $300 which he almost always does, I call. The turn is a five and he checks. Based on how he plays which consists of always raising pre-flop and always betting the flop, along with his turn check here, I think he doesn't have a queen. Since he is suspicious this is a good time to not trap and just bet straight away. Most people wouldn't be aggressive and bet a five, so when I bet I am saying I have a queen or am just making some weird bluff. He's not going to catch a good second best hand here so he has a decision to make about if I have something or not, and my bet looks more suspicious on the turn than on the river. On the turn it looks like I am just quickly trying to get him out so this is a good spot to not trap. In this case I bet $700 into a $900 pot and he check-raised all-in for $1,500 total with A-2.

Example 5

$25/$50 HU, opponent has $3,300 and is a tilting maniac. I raise to $150 on the button and he reraises to $450 and I call with 66. The flop is Q♣-7♠-6♥ and he has been betting the flop when he has something and check-folding when he doesn't have anything. And when I check behind he almost always automatically bets pot of $900 into me on the turn which he does here when the 8♥ comes. Now this puts an awful lot of draws out there and it's time to ask a couple of questions. What is his hand range? Very wide. What is the best way to get money out of that hand range? Because he is so aggressive and is currently betting, we want to let him keep the lead and let him be overaggressive. So the best play is to just call his bet. His hand range is so wide right now that it could be any two cards, and since he is a maniac he will give action on the river. He probably doesn't have a good hand that will give action now but might if a scare card comes. He probably doesn't even have that good of a draw. The plan is to call, and since he's a maniac we can't outguess ourselves on the river – it's a call no matter what card comes, even if it's the 9♥. In the hand a 10♦ fell off he went all in for $2,000 I called and he had Q-8.

Example 6

$10/$25 HU, opponent has $1,000 and I cover. I have J♣-3♥ and raise pre-flop to $75 and he calls. The flop is J♠-5♥-5♣ and he checks. We have top pair with no kicker and aren't too afraid of future cards coming to outdraw us as he probably has one overcard to hit at most. Granted future high cards could scare away action but that is a calculated risk. Also it's hard to put him on a second best hand that will give us action – the board wouldn't let that happen. If he hit the board it's either trip fives or a better pair of jacks. The situation is ripe for a trap.

In this particular case it turns out the best way to trap him is actually not to check. First of all, one problem with the check trap is he cannot catch a second best hand – he either pairs up to outdraw us or hits an under-pair which is such a weak hand he probably wouldn't commit much money with it. Here his stack size makes it easier – if he raises us if he does have us beat we stand to lose less. One of the reasons to normally check the flop is a combination of trapping and pot control as it would generally be bad to get 100 BB in here, however getting just 40 BB in is more reasonable.

The bottom line is that betting the flop is more suspicious than checking. Because the board is so dry and he couldn't have hit anything, it's also hard for us to have hit anything. And because this opponent is aggressive and loose I am alright to get all the money in here and so I bet $125, and he check-raised to $390 which makes things slightly awkward for us because once we call it shows we have an okay hand. For the turn play he would have the advantage as he would know about what type of hand we have and supposedly be able to play pretty close to correctly. We won't have a lot of flexibility given such good pot odds. However, with that being true, there is nothing we can do, we just will have to follow the plan. I called. The turn is a 3♠, he goes all-in and we call and his 10♠-4♠ is no good.

Example 7

$25/$50 three-handed, I have $7,500 and the opponent covers, he is bad player who is easy to read. He raises the button to $175 and I call with 2-2 in the BB. The flop is 2♣-6♠-7♥, I check and he bets $375 quickly. It has been a betting tell of his that when he bets full pot quickly he continues with a bet on the turn. I haven't seen his hands when he does this so it's unclear if it's a bluff or a good hand. In any case my only question here is how to build the biggest pot. The board is so uncoordinated that I'm not worried about draws – the only draws here are gutshot straight draws and an 8-9 but if he hits that there is nothing I can do so my main concern is just to build the pot.

So I called, the turn is the 2♠, I check and he quickly bets pot as expected. Now there are a couple of questions to ask – how often does he have a good hand here (an overpair) and how often is he bluffing and how often will he continue to bluff? My read was that he probably had a good hand but there was a chance he was bluffing. In either case I figured if I check-called there was a good chance he'd do it again on the river.

The river is the A♠ which seemed like the worst scare card possible and it became likely he would shut down now with whatever made hand he had. I considered leading out into him like $1,100 to force some value as he will be curious and suspicious and probably call – it's quite hard for people to fold a decent hand in a $3,500 pot for $1,100. However the deciding factor was his bet timing and sizing tell. When he had quickly bet full pot before he always had followed it up on the next street with a bet. In the hand I checked and he immediately went all in and his K-Jo lost.

Example 8

$25/$50 HU, opponent has $15,000 and I cover him. I have Q♣-8♣, he raises to $150 pre-flop and I call. The flop is A♣-K♣-5♠, I check he bets $300 and I call to mix it up. The turn is the Q♠, check-check. The river is the 10♣. This is a perfect time to check and trap. The reason is that I will only get money from the opponent if he has a straight or if he has a flush. So if he doesn't have one of those two hands it doesn't matter what the river action is, the result is always the same.

So let's say he has one of those two hands and consider what will happen if I check and what will happen if I bet. If he has a flush and I bet he will raise all-in, and if I check he will bet and call my check-raise all-in so I get all his money either way. So the only hand that matters for analysis now is the straight and what happens when he has a straight if I bet and what happens if I check? If I bet he will only call me, but if I check he will bet and then maybe call a check-raise so I might get two bets on the river. I checked and he checked behind with K-4, from which I would have got no value anyway.

Folding Strong Hands

Example 1

$50/$100 three-handed. My opponent, who is a relatively solid and unimaginative player opens to $350 on the button, I reraise in the BB to $1,100 with A-A , and he makes the surprising move of four-betting me to $3,400 quickly. Since it's so rare for him to four-bet, and because he is unimaginative his bet means a big hand. To be more precise, it doesn't even have to be a big hand – just a hand he thinks is big. Also given that he will have position on me post-flop, and also considering that he doesn't give excessive action post-flop unless he has a big hand, and finally considering that a call by me will give away almost as much information as raising, I should have just gone all in pre-flop.

But this time I just called. The flop came K-K-6, I checked and he bet $3,600. Now we must ask what the hand range from a tight uni-maginative player after this pre-flop action is – A-A, A-K, K-K or Q-Q. If he has queens he'll check the flop for sure – why would he bet them? He isn't calling a check-raise and he doesn't need to pro-tect his hand against outdraws, which would only have two or three outs. And he's not bluffing with nothing because his pre-flop action says he has a strong hand. Even given a small chance he was bluff-ing pre-flop, since I called he would probably give his bluff up and check the flop. So his hand range is basically A-K or K-K. I pushed foolishly and he instantly called with A-K. A rule of thumb is when you put in about 10% of your stack pre-flop with aces, it's okay to go to the felt with it all the time on the flop. That rule of thumb worked, and my flop play here is standard for almost everyone. However this was a great opportunity to make a big fold here and gain a lot of EV that other players wouldn't get.

Example 2

$50/$100 three-handed, $15,000 stacks. I have A-A and raise on the button to $350, opponent makes it $1,100 in the BB. He is passive and doesn't reraise much pre-flop. A lot of the time just calling with aces is a better play here because four-bets are really strong and let people fold their medium-strength hands and bluffs. However in this spot the opponent is probably quite strong because he never reraises pre-flop, so I four-bet to $3,500 and he calls. The flop comes 10♠-5♠-5♣, he checks. When most people get aces and reraise pre-flop one of two things happen – they get over excited and want to get all the opponent's money right away, or they get afraid of playing a tricky pot on later streets and instantly bet pot on the flop without realising that the easiest line is not always the most profitable. However, in this spot a bet is best as he didn't call with a weak hand with the intention of bluffing me out later – he has something strong and has to make a decision about whether I'm bluffing or not. Maybe I'll get his money, maybe I won't.

The other question to ask is what hands could I trap by checking,? Well not many – the only card that could come to set an effective trap is a king, and if he happens to have a king in his hand there are only three of those left. I'm not so afraid about the flush because there is only one exact hand combination that could have a flush draw – A♠-K♠. So I bet the pot of $6,500, he thinks for a while and goes-all in. I obviously call, as his hand range here is probably A-A – Q-Q, 10-10 or A♠-K♠. Also I'm getting 4-1 odds on my money, and this was my plan when I bet the flop. So I called and he had A♠-K♠.

If we consider his side of the things this hand will show us how not to play a draw. Reraising pre-flop is perfectly normal with A-Ks (though it would have been smart of him to reraise more frequently so I didn't put him on a hand range as narrow as Q-Q – A-A and A-K or A-Q). However, my four-bet is quite strong. One thing he should realize is that I am a better player than him, and he should give me respect and realize I can outplay him. If an ace flops he won't get bluffs from me and if it doesn't I'll push him off his hand.

An ace or king will only flop 1/3 times and he's out of position. He needs to give a better player his due and fold A-K here.

Example 3

$10/$25 HU, opponent raises to $75 on the button and I call with 9♠-10♠. The flop is 8♥-3♦-2♠, check-check. The turn is the 9♦ which makes for a lot of hands composed of some combination of straight draw and overcard draw that he'll semi-bluff there. Here he checked, then the river comes the A♠. I check and he bets $150. It's pretty frustrating that he checked behind on the turn then such a bad card comes on the river and it's very easy to call here out of a combination of frustration and curiosity at what he has, hoping that our hand is good. But this is actually a good spot in a small pot to fold where most people would make a sloppy call and lose their $150. Part of the reason is that one of the most likely hands the opponent checks behind on the flop and turn is ace high – it has showdown value so he doesn't need to bluff with it like he would with a hand like K-J.

Example 4

$25/$50 four-handed, button raises to $175, SB calls and I call in the BB with A-5s. The flop is 2♠-6♠-K♣ and to mix it up I lead out $500. The button calls and the turn comes the 10♥, I check, the pot is $1,500 and he bets $1,300. Should I check-raise my last $3,000? Or call? No, even though I have the ace-high flush draw with an overcard it's a fold. It's very hard for me to have two pair here with the flop being so uncoordinated – I could have hit two pair on the turn with K-10, but K-10 I wouldn't lead the flop.

Therefore my flop lead is either air, a flush draw, or a set. When I check-raise the turn all-in he can put me on either a flush draw or a set. The fact is sets don't come along as often as flush draw so the question is whether he a weak player who sees a big bet and automatically folds one pair? Or is he a thinking player who will put his money in when he thinks his hand is best? In this case I thought he was just a loose suspicious bad player, so I just folded which is the best play on the turn.

Example 5

$10/$25 HU, opponent is playing weird illogical poker, he is tricky and a little tough to play but has many leaks. He changes his bet size a lot making small and medium bets with small hands and bluffs and he bets full pot when he has a good hand. I raise pre-flop to $75 with Q-J and he calls. The flop is Q-7-2, and he check-calls a bet of $150. He calls a fair amount. The turn is a two and in terms of pot size my hand is good enough to get one more bet into the pot. But if we go all-in, or bets go in on both the turn and river then there's a good chance I'll lose.

Therefore I check the turn and hope to get value on the river. The river is an eight and he leads out $400 like he does with good hands. I was slowly grinding this player down so strategically it's not bad to fold here. Also, I had a feeling he wasn't bluffing which came from the game tempo, his bet size and bet speed. Another reason it probably isn't a bluff is because there isn't anything for his bluff to represent. No scare cards hit and I either have a pair of queens or I don't. If I have a pair of queens I'm probably calling any bet up to the pot size. If my hand is worse than a pair of queen than I'm probably folding to about a 3/4 pot bet or even a little less. So he can accomplish the same bluff by betting about $300 – but he didn't, he bet $400. My read was that he's targeting me if I have a queen and so I folded.

Example 6

$25/$50, four-handed. I open on the button with Q-Jo to $175, the SB raises to $575, BB folds and I call. This is normally a fold but he is playing aggressive and people are pushing me around pre-flop. The flop is K♣-Q♠-7♠ and he leads out $725. Since I called with such a marginal hand, the situation is marginal and I have to play very well to make it an okay call pre-flop. Although, just because I called pre-flop doesn't mean that if I hit something I am committed to putting money into the pot – I called his reraise pre-flop so the Q and K are very likely cards to have hit me and his bet size seems to say that he wants to keep me in the pot. We can't know for sure but it looks like he is targeting us if we have a queen. What I mean is if we have a pair of kings we are probably going to put money into the pot whether he bets $725 or if he bets $1,150. If we have 10-10 or Q-J we are probably not going to put money in if he bets the full pot $1,150, however we are more likely to put money in if he bets smaller.

The first piece of evidence is he bet on a board that could very likely hit a person calling a reraise pre-flop. The second piece of evidence is that he bet small like he's trying to trap us. Normally a small bet is evidence of weakness but here it's different because given the board texture it's quite likely we hit something. And if we hit something and he bet small it looks like he's wanting us to call and if he wants us to call that means he has a good hand and should fold. Also this player is aggressive and when he bets the flop he generally bets the turn, so for that reason we need to make a decision here as to whether we are willing to go all-in with a pair queens on the turn when he bets, and that simply can't be justified as he is aggressive but not a maniac.

Bet-call and check-call lines with weak hands

Example 1

$10/$25 six-handed, two folds and a limper, I raise pot to $110 with K♥-10♥, SB calls and so does limper. I have $2,400 and limper covers me. The flop is K♣-5♠-Q♥, SB checks and BB leads out into me for

$250. I call and the SB folds, the turn comes the 4♦ and he leads out $600. Now we have a decision to make and now it's time to start hand reading.

Normally according to the basic concepts of poker this is a fold – it was a three-way pot pre-flop, we have top pair and a kicker that isn't worth much and the opponent has made a decent sized turn bet and is certainly threatening to make a big river bet. Normally we don't play top pair for big pots, let alone 100 BB. And had I been playing on autopilot without consciously and deliberately thinking through the hand I surely would have folded. But doing exactly that yields interesting results. Try putting him on a specific hand. A set? K-K is very unlikely as there is exactly one combination since I have a king and there is a king on the board, Q-Q is unlikely either because he limp-called pre-flop, and for the same reason he doesn't have aces. He also doesn't have A-K because he wouldn't limp call with it pre-flop.

K-J is a possibility but this line with K-J would be quite peculiar as his hand isn't quite good enough to be played so aggressively. K-Q he probably would just raise pre-flop but assuming he limp called he probably wouldn't lead out on the flop since he has the board dominated. He could have a set of fives but that is only one hand combination so not too likely. Therefore since we can't put him a set we will continue with K-10 but should we raise or fold? Raising makes no sense as if he is bluffing we want him to keep bluffing and the board isn't too scary with draws so we don't need to raise for protection. The only reason to raise would be if we are very sure he has a draw and also very sure he will not bluff us on the river. So we call, the river is a queen and he goes all-in. Now we must ask if there is anyway he could have a queen? Not really, he would have had to bet the flop and the turn with a Q somehow like A-Q, K-Q or Q-5 which don't make sense. So I call and he shows 8-6 for a gutshot draw he picked up on the turn.

Example 2

$10/25 HU, the opponent has $1,350 and I cover. I have 99, he raises on the button to $75 and I reraise to $225. He calls. The pot is $450 and he has $1,100 left, the flop is K♥-8♠-2♣. Now normally pot control would be a huge factor here as you would be trying to keep the pot small because if the pot got big and you went to a showdown you would likely lose. In this particular case however, the opponent is raising very frequently and calling all reraises. So in general pocket nines are a good hand and will often still be best on the flop. This flop is also relatively good with just one overcard so since he is so loose and tilting and our nines are probably the best hand we just have to get the money in and see what happens.

Therefore I bet $325 and he calls. The turn is the 7♠, I check because if he floated the flop with nothing or a weak hand just to see what I'd do, I want to give him a chance to bluff here. He went all-in, I called and he had 56. In this hand he could very easily have had us beat but sometimes in poker there is nothing you can do to avoid losing money and this would have been one of those spots.

Example 3

$25/50 HU, opponent is very loose-aggressive and bad. He is raising almost every button and then almost always continuation betting the flop, he has $2,500 and I cover. He raises pre-flop and I call with K-10s. The opponent is so bad and needlessly aggressive that I can just wait to see if I hit a flop with this hand, and then get the money in from there because he will always bet. So here I call, the flop is K-9-3, I check and he bets $300 as expected. Now normally I have top pair with a medium kicker and it's not good to get 50 BBs in on the flop with that on a dry board. A good player would either check behind on the flop with something like K-5 so he can practice pot control himself, or he'd fold it pre-flop, or if someone raised him he'd make a good decision. This particular opponent will not only bet the flop with K-5, always raise it pre-flop and will make a bad decision if I raise, but he could be betting any two cards and will call with worse kings. So instead of calling which I'd normally do, in this case I check-raised to $1,000, he immediately went all-in and his K-4 lost.

Example 4

$10/$25 HU, opponent is very bad and loose-passive, he has already been stacked a couple of times. I raise K-Qo to $75 and he calls. The flop is 4♦-4♠-6♦, he check-calls a $125 bet. The turn is the 6♥ and he checks, I check behind. The pot is $450, the river comes an off-suit Jack and he leads out $270. My instincts told me that something felt off – there was a combination of factors here that made his play suspicious. He plays straightforward, so if he hit the six on the turn he probably would have led out and so far he has bet the full pot instantly with hands he likes and he didn't do that here, which is evidence he doesn't like his hand. He calls me pre-flop almost every time so his hand range is wide, and he calls my flop bets very often too, so his hand range is wide there too. If he had ace high he would probably check the river because ace high has showdown value. With A-4 in his hand he would raise the flop. A-6 would probably bet the pot on the river. The combination of all these factors made me suspicious so I called and he had 5-2. It's worth noting that a raise is bad as if he has a 4 or a 6 he is never folding. The worst hand he could have is a jack and a raise is so suspicious and he's so bad that he could call anyway.

Example 5

$10/$25 HU, opponent is a clown but plays like a nit so it's a grind to take his money away. He min-raises on the button, I re-pop to $150 with 8-8 and he calls. This sequence has happened a few times already. He is short-stacked with $1,200. The flop is A♣-10♦-2♣, and I check as there is no reason to bet. He checks too. The turn is the Q♠, I check and he checks. The river is the 4♣, I check and he bets $300.

Normally this is an easy fold just based on the obvious fact that it is an underpair to a board with three overcards in a re-raised pot.

But my instincts said his bet doesn't make sense. His pre-flop range is wide as he raised pre-flop a lot and would always call my reraise. Then if he has a big hand why wouldn't he bet the flop or turn both for value and to protect it. Then the river is a blank so it doesn't change the strength of his hand and he chose that time to bet? He bets full pot too which on that board indicates a good amount of strength which is inconsistent with the facts, so this is suspicious. Also, it indicates a lot of strength because he was not a sophisticated opponent so if he bets full pot it's not with a medium strength hand mixing it up and he is not sophisticated enough to trap by checking the flop and turn with a good hand that often. Even given all of these factors it is still a hard call to make given the board and the weakness of my hand but in HU poker and you can't let scare cards get to you and you can't let yourself get run over. I called and he had 6♥-9♥.

Example 6

$10/$25, same opponent, he has $1,300 and I cover. He limps on the button, I raise with K-K to $75, he calls. The flop is J♣-10♦-3♥, I bet $150 and he calls. The turn is the 7♥ and it felt like he would fold if I bet and he might bet so I checked hoping to check-raise but he checks behind. The river is the 8♥. I check and he quickly bets $450. Again my instincts said his bet was off partly because of his bet timing. But it's also based on straight forward hand analysis too. He could have a flush but this is a backdoor flush and those are hard to come by HU. He could have a straight but that means very specific hands for him like 10-9 or J-9 or Q-9. The big question is how sophisticated he is, e.g. would he bet two pair on the river against me to get value? A tough player would bet many two pair hands on the river as well as a flush or a straight so his hand range is a lot wider. But in this case the opponent isn't sophisticated and would only bet a straight or flush or a bluff, which makes it a lot more likely I'm ahead. I called and he had 53.

Example 7

$10/25 six-handed, I raise in MP with A♥-9♥ to $85 and only the SB calls. The flop is 3♣-10♦-2♦, check-check. The turn is the 4♠, check-check. The river is the 7♦ and the opponent quickly leads out the pot. What is he representing? Well he didn't bet on the flop or the turn so based on that it doesn't seem that strong. And if he had a medium to weak made hand wouldn't he check the river and hope for a free showdown? So he's representing a flush, but people don't get flushes all that often – additionally he might be betting with that on the turn. I called and he had Q♠-J♠.

Example 8

$5/$10 HU, opponent has $400 and I cover, he is bad and loose. I have A♠-5♠ and raise on the button to $30, he calls. The flop is 5♥-9♠-6♦, he checks. In NLHE it can be hard to protect your hand sometimes – for instance if we bet the pot of $60 then he will not call with worse hands but he could bluff or semi-bluff us and he can call with better hands. And if we changed our bet size to protect the pot to something like $20 then it would give a lot of information away about the type of hand we have and he could outplay us. So normally to be deceptive we are forced to check in this situation. However given that he is especially bad here I bet $25 for the purpose of protecting my hand since he is so bad he won't be able to take advantage of my obvious bet size.

He called and its unclear what he has at this point. The turn is the 3♦, he checks and I check behind. The river is the 9♦ and he leads out $110 quickly. Let's do some hand reading – he quickly bet out the pot so he's representing a good hand, which here would be a flush or a nine. Its not likely that he back-doored a flush so does he have a nine? Well, because we bet so small on the flop his flop call does not prove to us that he has a nine. And particularly in light of the fact that he's so bad and part of the reason we bet $25 is because he's capable of calling it with garbage. Things get a little trickier if his hand range expands to include a pair of sixes because that expands his range significantly and makes it more likely he has one of the hands that he could be playing it that way that beats us. Fortunately this player is not sophisticated enough to make such aggressive value bets with weak hands. I called and he had J-Qo

Changing gears

Changing gears has a lot to do with being in the 'zone'. The question is are you focusing on the poker game, or mindlessly playing standard poker? If it's the latter then you're in trouble. You might be doing fine but then cards will fall a certain way – for instance you get a few good hands in a row and raise the opponent and he folds. Now he doesn't know you had good hands each time – in fact he'll be pretty sure you didn't have it one of those times because mathematically that is the most likely scenario by far. And if you raise him again soon he'll be even more sure you are bluffing, thus you need to adjust. Your standard system of play isn't going to work in this situation because an odd run of cards has your opponent suspicious and he is going to adjust, so you need to adjust to that adjustment – and that is what changing gears is about.

Example 1

$10/$25 HU, opponent has $2,200 and I cover. I open to $75 with A-K and he calls. The flop is A♠-K♦-10♦ and he check-calls my pot bet of $150. The turn is the 5♣ and he checks. If he has some sort of draw or made hand draw combination I want to entice him to continue the hand and also entice him to do so on terms unfavorable to him so I bet $300 here and he calls.

The river is the 3♣ and he leads out the full pot for $1,050 and my initial happiness and confidence about the hand quickly went away. My hand was so strong that I had to call, but the decision was either to call or go all-in. In a spot like this where his bet really surprised me it's easy to let that affect my decision and make me call or go all-in without thinking. But don't do that – be meticulous, think and hand read.

He seems to be representing a strong hand but no really strong hands make sense here. The issue is that if he has a straight or a set from the start his hand is strong but vulnerable and so he would have raised at some point. Action like this could be a pocket pair that hit a set on the river but there is no way he could have called the flop and turn with 3-3. One hand that does make sense is A-3, but fortunately we beat that hand.. So in the end it's impossible to put him on a hand that beats us, so we raise all-in. He called with A-4.

Example 2

A couple of hands after that the opponent is playing with a $1,200 stack. I raise the button to $75 with Q-8o and he reraises to $195. Normally this is an easy fold, but given his complete recklessness and the fact that I have position and that he didn't make a full pot raise it makes sense to call here and see what develops. I call, the flop is K-8-7o and he quickly bets out the pot of $390. Again this is normally a spot where people lose a lot of money by getting dragged into a hand early on, and then when they hit a hand they think they have to go with it.

Well I don't have to go with it given his quick full sized pot bet felt strong to me and the king is one of the worst cards that could come. Also the stack sizes make it awkward. However the most profitable play is not always the easiest play and that is the case here. The simple fact is that his previous play with A-4 was just so crazy and he lost his whole stack, so he could be tilting even more here and that makes it a call. I called and without putting anymore money into the pot won against his 9-4o.

Miscellaneous

Example 1

$25/50 six-handed, button raises to $175, the SB calls and I call in the BB with 8-9o. The flop is A♥-9♥-4♠, it is checked around. The turn is the 6♣ and the SB leads out for $400. This is a peculiar bet from him because when he has a good hand he has bet the pot in the past. A lot of the times people will bet smaller with their best hands but short-handed people rarely make huge hands. Basically, there are a lot of different hands he could have but because of his bet size it doesn't feel strong. Another factor is the math. Some people in this spot will bet out and you'll bluff-raise and they'll always seem to have a good hand. Other people will fold often. The key to seeing how often they have a big hand or not is how often they call pre-flop. If they rarely call then they are already filtering their hand selection, so if they bet the flop often and have it often, it's because pre-flop they already dumped the trash. If they call pre-flop a lot then bet the flop frequently they are going to have many weak holdings.

Now, all three options are viable here. I could certainly fold – some opponents are suspicious and some are weak. This particular opponent is weak and doesn't put up much of a fight with mediocre holdings. I could call but he could have a lot of mediocre hands that still beat me, and there is also a player behind me. Also, he could bluff the river if I call. If I raise he'll have a hard time calling with his mediocre holdings. Also if he does show up with a hand I probably have outs. Plus if I'm a better player then I can raise and if he calls, I can plan on outplaying him based on his timing, the river card, and his river action. Another advantage is that he could call with a draw which is the best of both worlds. My decision to raise here is a combination of many marginal factors, and the play itself is quite marginal but it illustrates the thinking behind this sort of play.

Example 2

$3/$6 six-handed, UTG raises to $21, I call with red jacks in the SB and it's HU. The flop is A♥-10♥-9♥, I check and he bets pot for $46. The opponent is a decent player who is giving me a lot of respect and this is a good time to use that respect to end this pot right now instead of playing more streets out of position, which will get confusing. A raise is good here because if we just call we will not know exactly where we stand in the hand and it makes playing future streets uncertain and confusing. If the opponent has an ace without a heart we can also bluff him. Also, after a check-raise we could get a free turn card even though we're out of position.

Example 3

$25/$50 HU, I raise on the button with A-Ko and my opponent calls which he does often, we have $5k stacks. The flop is 3-5-10, he checks. Normally always continuation betting Ace high here is a leak because people can simply call with better or fold worse hands but a few factors in combination made it a bet against this player. He calls the flop quite often, so it could be a value bet against a weak ace or some weird hand he wants to float with. Also he is passive, so if I bet he probably won't check-raise the flop and I can get to see two more cards if I want by checking behind on the turn, and I can choose the bet size. And finally he calls the flop a lot but is weak on the turn and has folded to many continuation bets, so if the turn card is scary I can keep bluffing. In the hand he called, the turn was a Q, and he folded to my turn bet.

Example 4

$5/$10 six-handed, two limpers and hero raises to $55 with A-A , one limper calls. The flop is 9♦-J♥-8♥ (hero doesn't have A♥). villain checks to hero. What plan does he have here, what sort of pot does he want? On the flop he most certainly wants a small one. The problem is if the villain has a piece of this board he is somewhere around even money to beat A-A on the flop and if he has a big piece of the board then he crushes the hero, so there isn't a lot of value in betting this flop

So if the opponent has nothing our action doesn't matter because he only has a few outs to outdraw our aces and supposing he isn't a better player than us, he probably won't be able to bluff us out. So if we bet and he has nothing, he'll fold and if we check and he has nothing we'll just win the hand on a later street and our action doesn't matter. And if the opponent has a very strong hands then checking is good because we aren't putting money into the pot against it.

The reason why this hand is so tricky and why checking has value is if the opponent has a strong draw. If the opponent has a strong draw he can raise us as a semi-bluff on the flop and we'll have to fold because on this board the villain wouldn't go all-in with nothing. So we gain a lot more equity by waiting for the turn to see if our aces are still good, and we can see what his action is because we have position

If you were the opponent and had middle set here you probable want to lead out and do the betting yourself, since a top pair/overpair hand will usually check behind here, or bet with the intention of folding to a raise. Value betting top pair is dubious on this board because hands worse than top pair can't call very often but if the pot stays small top pair has a better chance of being the best hand. Of course, this is all highly situational depending on the way the game is playing and the opponent but this illustrates the way you should be thinking about hands.

Example 5

$25/$50 HU, opponent has $7,500 and I cover. I have A-6o and raise to $150, he calls. The flop is 4♥-6♠-8♣, he checks, I bet $225 and he check-raises to $525. I'm not sure exactly what's going on at this point but I'm a lot better then the opponent with position and can outplay him, and also he is not a nit and there's a good chance he doesn't have a big hand so I call. The turn is the 2♠, he bets $475 into the $1,350 pot and his bet size gives the game away as when he bets small he is weak so I raise to $1,900 and take the pot down.

Heads-up matches

Finally here are complete hand histories and commentary from three heads-up matches. A couple of notes here. You'll see that I don't play perfectly and I'll make no attempt to hide it – no one does. Even when someone is playing their best poker they are still making a lot of sub-optimal plays, which is part of the beauty of the game – the fact that everyone always plays bad in comparison to the "perfect game" means that there is always room to play better and earn more money.

It's impossible to analyze poker hands and come to definite conclusions about what was a good play, what was a bad play, and by how much was it good or bad. The value of this section is not so much in the final judgments I make and the corresponding good or bad plays that occur but in seeing all the factors that enter into a decision. Then you can take all the concepts involved and start weighing them into your own decisions in, and over time with much study and repetition your judgment will improve.

Another point is that everyone plays different. It is another beautiful part of HU poker that it allows for people to play in extremely different ways and still be skilled and win money. For this reason also it's important to focus not so much on the specifics of the lines I take but on the thought processes and ideas behind what is happening.

Heads-up match #1, $25/50, $5,000 starting stacks

Hand 1

I open on the button to $150 with 8♣-7♣, the opponent reraises to $450. It's the first hand and he reraised which makes me suspicious so far based on the facts that he is loose and aggressive. However even with that being so it's a bit suspect to put in 10% of my stack pre-flop with low cards, even if they are suited connectors. To put in so much pre-flop we generally want high cards, and of course hopefully suited and/or connected ones. However I felt like gambling a bit and since the decision is close it really doesn't matter too much one way or the other. If I call it will lead to a looser gambling game with big pots and higher variance, and if I fold it will be a smaller pot game with less variance.

I call and the flop comes A♥-J♠-8♠ and he leads out $900, and I fold. Just because I have a pair doesn't mean I need to go with it. He reraised preflop representing high cards, then the flop comes with high cards and he continues to represent his good hand by betting the pot on the flop. I believe him and even if I didn't it would be a lot of money to commit in a very precarious position, so the flop fold is straightforward.

Hand 2

Opponent on button folds. This is pretty common point about game tempo actually. After winning a big pot like that the opponent will fold pre-flop the next hand more often than they would normally.

Hand 3

I raise 7-9o to $150, he calls. Flop is J♦-Q♣-8♦, he checks and I check.

I want to wait for the turn to gain more information before risking a bluff. Also if he calls it's likely I have no overcards and just a gutshot draw to hit a ten which has no implied odds because it's so obvious. Also it's a bad board texture to bluff because if the opponent has a has a hand there's a higher chance then normal it's a decent hand with outs. For instance on a more normal looking board like K-J-6 if the opponent had 6-7 it's just bottom pair, but in the actual hand if the opponent has bottom pair with something like 8-9 or 8-10 he also has a gutshot draw and can continue more readily. Similarly compare how J-10 works on both boards. If we bluffed the flop on the K-J-6 board he'll call, then say the turn is a two. If we bet again he'll probably fold even if he's suspicious we're bluffing as it's hard for him to call because he has no outs. However on the Q-J-8 board if we bet the flop and he calls then the turn is a two and we bet again and he's suspicious, it's a lot easier for him to call because he has outs. So the board texture takes away some of our options.

The turn comes the 7♠, he checks. Now it's not worth it to bluff. Before we paired the sevens a bet would make sense to make him fold ace high, king high, and pairs below sevens. Now if we bluff we have to make him fold hands better than a pair of sevens to be worth it. And the only hand out of those he'd fold is probably a pair of eights. So we check and also give ourselves a chance to improve our hand. River is the 5♦ and he leads out $50. At this point if we raise him our hand does not represent anything. We checked the flop and turn showing weakness and the river card doesn't change the board. So the way to interpret it, is one of two things. Either a stupid bet that makes no sense with ace high or some random hand – in which case simply calling is the best course of action. Or as a made hand that knows we are weak and is trying to extract $50 of value and might even hope we raise as a bluff, because he knows we are weak and will call the raise. I called, he had K-J.

Hand 4

He raises to $150, we call with Q-10o. This is a good hand to mix it up and reraise because we have two relatively high cards to pair, and also can take it down pre-flop, however it feels like this is the type of opponent who will call a lot. If he'll call the reraise a lot this play loses a lot of it's value. The flop is A♠-Q♣-7♥, I check and he checks. Turn is 3♠, I check and he checks. If you felt the need to put money into the pot on the flop or turn simply ask yourself what will it accomplish? What hands is he going to call, and what will he fold, and how does that help you? The river comes the K♣, and if the card was a rag my plan had been to value bet because he checked twice so he doesn't have an ace. Now the king scares him if he has a worse hand so he won't call, and also he could have very easily hit that king. Check-check, he has 8-8.

Hand 5

I raise to $150 with K-10o, he folds.

Hand 6

He folds.

Hand 7

I raise to $150 with A-10o, he folds. This is the sort of opponent I like. If he keeps this up it's so easy to play versus him. His hand range is smaller, he's predictable. I won't need to force anything post-flop because I can make an easy profit pre-flop against him.

Hand 8

He min-raises to $100, again this weird play reinforces my belief that started to grow from the last hand. This is a poor play pre-flop which is easy for me to play against as he isn't putting much pressure on me with a min-raise. He can make up for it with better post-flop play but it's a good sign for me. I call with A-8o. Flop is 3♦-5♦-K♠, check-check. Turn is 7♠, check-check. Maybe a bet is good here but it's early on in the game, I don't have much of a read on the opponent and don't know what his flop check means so I'll take it slow and check. River is the Q♣, again a bet here is probably good but I made a mistake and let the inertia take over from the turn. I checked the turn so it's easy to check the river too, it's also particularly easy to check since our hand has a little bit of showdown value which allows us to be lazy. This shows how you have to always be alert and this is very important as a player. He checked behind and won with 2-2.

Hand 9

I raise with J-9o and he folds.

Hand 10

He folds. Looking good for me.

Hand 11

I raise to $150 with A-Ko, he calls. He has folded a lot pre-flop so it's sometimes tempting to limp and trap him. But limping doesn't build a big pot, A-K has the potential to win a big pot so even if he folds a lot pre-flop we have to risk it to try and achieve the potential of A-K here. The flop is 9♣-10♣-Q♠, he leads out $50. Not sure what this means, but I think it's weak. If I call and he leads out on the turn on a rag then things get awkward to play. Here after a $50 bet he's probably not going to three-bet me so I don't need to worry about missing my drawing chances. A big part of the reason I raise here is that if he calls, I will check behind on the turn and take another card for free. He folded to the pot raise.

Hand 12

Opponent folds. At this point he's playing bad. First of all it's very unlikely he hasn't had a hand good enough to raise pre-flop. And secondly even if all of his hands are 2-6o (which they aren't), he can still raise as he can use his position and his growing image as a tight player to do that.

Hand 13

I raise A-6o, he folds.

Hand 14

Opponent raises to $150, I have 8-10o. It's so easy to play against him there is no need to mix it up for strategic reasons with a hand like 8-10o out of position so I folded.

Hand 15

8-2o, I fold. Raising is probably profitable here but I've raised every hand so far and he keeps folding. I like the way he's playing which is tight and bad, and don't want to change it by raising every hand. So I fold marginally profitable hands that could raise like here.

Hand 16

He raises to $150, I fold 7-2o.

Hand 17

I raise 4-5s he folds.

Hand 18

He limps and I check with K-8, although in all likelihood if I raised to $250 here he would probably fold so that is valid to consider. The flop is A♥-A♠-K♦, I check and he checks. Turn is the 7♠, and here perhaps a bet would be good, because he doesn't appear to bluff and semi-bluff much. The river is the 9♥, and again he doesn't seem like a bluffer or even an aggressive value bettor, so here I bet out $50 and he folded.

Hand 19

I have 8-Qo and raise to $150, he calls. Flop is 2♦-4♠-5♥, he checks, I check. Turn is the 6♣, he checks. A bet here by me is kind of suspicious because what am I representing, a straight? First of all I need to have raised pre-flop and have exactly that card in my hand to make a straight. But also I probably would have bet the flop if I had the three as a semi-bluff, which all makes a turn bet rather odd by me. But as stated above he appears to play pretty straightforwardly, and he doesn't seem to hand read and play suspiciously, so I go ahead and bet $300 and he folds.

Hand 20

He limps, I check with A-3o. The flop is 7♠-A♠-6♣, I checked the flop which is the standard play here because the BB didn't commit any money to the pot pre-flop so I have a completely random hand which is supposedly bad and doesn't contain an ace. As SB he limped and is more likely to have an ace, and thus represent an ace. That is why checking is the standard play, however as stated this opponent is either too lazy or uncreative to represent hands so in this case betting the flop and trying to get value when he has a lower pair or even when he does something weird like try and float me with 8-10 or 5-9 would be ok

But in the hand I checked, he bet $100 and I called. The turn is the 8♥,

I check and he bets $300. Given how little aggression he has shown so far and given the fact that I have no redraws, and that even if he doesn't have me beat he most likely is semi-bluffing with redraws, and given that it was unraised pre-flop this is a pretty easy fold. Originally our plan was to trap him, but that changed. It's a tough road to walk because once we show weakness it's important not to get bluffed out because that's exactly what we tried to induce the opponent to do. But on the other hand by trapping with a weak hand we might just be trapping ourselves. Versus an opponent I respected I'd probably call him down and follow through with the plan, not giving myself a chance to outguess myself and be outplayed. But versus a bad player like this opponent, I am confident in my ability to read his hands and not afraid of outguessing myself.

Hand 21

4-8o. In retrospect perhaps this is a raise by me but I folded in the game. He had just won the previous hand, and often when people win a hand they loosen up a bit with their extra money and confidence and for that reason I folded.

Hand 22

3♥-9♥, he raises, I fold. Note we've played 22 hands already and there hasn't been a big pot – that is the way games go sometimes. Don't force big pots, patience and precision is the key.

Hand 23

10-2o, I folded and in retrospect this is almost certainly a mistake given how much he folds to my pre-flop raises and how straightforwardly he plays post-flop. This is an example of the opponent having the momentum and it getting me off balance and playing defensively.

Hand 24

Opponent limps, I check with Q♥-3♥. Note before he went through a cycle where he folded a few hands in a row, and now he likes to limp – this is probably because he has won a few pots in a row and has the momentum. HU poker is very much a game of having momentum and the psychological advantage. The flop is 7♠-J♣-K♦, we both check. Turn is the 4♣, I check and he checks. River is the 5♥, I check and he checks and wins with 5-6. The fact that he checks behind on the turn with a hand that has no showdown value but is great for building a pot or taking the pot down there is evidence he is passive, and evidence he is a bad player.

Hand 25

2♦-9♦, I limp and he checks. The flop is 5♣-J♠-5♦, he checks and I bet $100. Against a tricky opponent I'd be more likely to bet $200 because the bigger bet size is more likely to deter him from floating or raising me with wacky hands (which he'd be correct to do), however this opponent doesn't see my bet size and the board and think what he can do to me. He sees he has no hand, and simply that I placed a bet and folds.

Hand 26

He folds.

Hand 27

I have A♥-4♥ and raise to $150, he calls. The flop is A♦-6♥-9♥ and this is sometimes a good spot to trap, the idea being that if I bet now I'll force him out when he has weaker hands and build the pot when he has a better hand than me. And if he has a good hand I should just check and wait until I hit my hand and build the pot then. However against this type of player who isn't going to go wild if I hit a flush and he has a lesser hand, and who isn't going to get too aggressive when I show signs of weakness on the flop, it's better just to bet straight out. I bet a little less than pot, $235, to give him room to stay in there with weaker hands, but he folds.

Hand 28

He limps, I raise to $150 with Q♥-J♠. He seems pretty straightforward post-flop so it's okay to raise out of position. Q-Jo is a better hand than what he has so it's a raise for value. The flop is A♦-9♠-7♠, I check and he bets $300. I figured he would have raised pre-flop if he had an ace in his hand, thus that makes his bet a bluff probably. So I raised him to $1,200. However given his reluctance to make bluffs before this I should have given him credit for a hand that I was unable to put him on, just because he doesn't seem to bluff. He called.

The turn is the 3♠. Now this is an interesting time to bet for sure as I think he gives me respect, so if he has a pair of aces he will fold them. However if he has a pair of aces and a spade then he'll probably call. The pot is $1,500, so if I bet say $1,300 and he calls then the pot becomes $4,000 and he will have $3,000 left and so will I. So given the pot size and stack sizes it becomes quite natural for him to raise me all-in which will scare me or fold, and less likely for him to simply call. This changes my play from a semi-bluff (with my J♠) to a bluff, which might be okay but is a tough decision. I checked and so did he. The river is the 2♠ and the action I probably want vs. this opponent is check-check and I win the showdown, which is what happened. He showed 8-6o.

Hand 29

Opponent now has $3,750 and I cover. I have K-K and raise to $150, he calls. Flop is 8♣-5♦-2♦. At the time I was hoping he was tilting from the last hand and would overplay his hand if he had something here and bet out $300 when he checked to me, but he folded.

To be considered is that he probably has two overcards, so I could give him a free card to trap him. However that has disadvantages as he has to hit a six outer to trap himself and then we only have two streets to build a pot. If I bet the flop and he decides to overplay his hand then his whole stack is gone which is what I was hoping for and the right thing to do here. Here the game broke up.

Heads-up match #2, $25/50 vs. maniac, $5,000 starting stacks

Hand 1

I raise to $150 with A♥-5♥, opponent calls. Flop is 9♣-J♥-10♦, he checks and I check. It's easy for him to have a hand. Turn is the 9♦, check-check. River is the A♠ and he bets $300. He appears to be happy with his hand and he could very well have checked a good hand on the flop or turn to trap me. But it's hard to put him on a specific hand that beats me and importantly if he has a pair of aces to have a better kicker he needs A-K or A-Q which he'd reraise pre-flop – with all other pairs of aces we split the pot. I call, he has J-Q. His river bet simply makes no sense. So at this point I will be playing under the assumption he's bad.

Hand 2

K♦-8♦, opponent raises to $150, I call. The flop is K♠-8♣-5♦, since he appears to be crazy there is no need to take the lead away from him, especially since I dominate the board. I check, he checks. Turn is the 5♠, a bad card as it could make him a better hand, decreases the strength of mine, and most important of all, doesn't improve his hand. I check, he checks. River is the 2♣, I bet $300, he folded.

Hand 3

Q♣-2♥, I raise to $150. It's a marginal hand but it's the beginning of the game and I want to establish myself as aggressive and take the lead in the game. He calls, flop is 6♦-4♦-8♦. Here I figured since it looks like he is the type of opponent that calls everything pre-flop, he probably doesn't have a good hand here. And even though I don't have anything he wouldn't be able to stand a bet. So I bet $300 but he called. I guess that was a mistake as he appears to be the type of opponent that not only calls everything pre-flop but then is also crazy post-flop.

The turn comes the A♠. Then I figured that if he is crazy pre-flop and on the flop that means he still probably doesn't have a hand, the board is scary and the turn is a scare card. So I will go ahead and play more aggressively than him to muscle him out of the hand and here I bet pot for $900. It's quite possible for two opponents to be loose and aggressive and skilled, and then some pretty wacky hands can happen quite frequently. It involves a lot of aggression, bluffing, semi-bluffing and close decisions. That's what I was forcing myself into here, although it turns out the opponent is not skilled so strategically I didn't need to force these tough high variance decisions. He is loose and aggressive but not so skilled so I can just wait. In the hand he raised me to $1,800 and won the pot.

Hand 4

He raises to $150, I fold K-2o.

Hand 5

I raise $150 with 2-2, he folds.

Hand 6

He raises to $150, I reraise to $450 with A-Qo. This is a standard re-raise for value because my hand is far better than his range of hands. The flop is 8♠-K♦-2♥, I bet $700 because since he appears to be wacky it will be tough to try and showdown ace high and win the hand, and so I want to bet and end it right away. He would try and steal it from me at some point if I checked and then if I wanted to fight him for it I'd have to put in significantly more than $700 to fight for the pot. He calls.

The turn is the 6♥, I check and he checks. Since he didn't raise the flop or bet the turn, there is a pretty decent chance he doesn't have a king. But the combination of the fact that he might have a king, and that he might call a river bluff even without a king makes my plan to check down and lose the pot. The river comes a queen. It's close and I want to bet but given that we've only played six hands so far my read doesn't seem strong enough to justify making such a thin value bet. The pot is pretty big by now, I reraised pre-flop and bet the flop and he called that, so if I'm going to bet the river it's going to be a sizeable bet and if I'm wrong quite costly. I checked and he checked behind 8-9s.

Hand 7

I fold 5-2o.

Hand 8

He raises to $150, I call with J-9o. The flop is A♣-2♣-3♠, I check and he bets $300. He's too aggressive for me to sit back and wait around, and this is a good spot. My read is that he raises a lot pre-flop, so there's a quite good chance he doesn't have an ace in his hand. And he will need an ace to continue vs. me if I raise. So I am playing the math here and raise him to $1,000, he folds.

Hand 9

I raise Q-3s and he reraises pot, I fold.

Hand 10

He raises to $150, I call with Q-9o. I think he is loose and a suspicious type that will float me when I bet with weak hands so I lead out into him on the flop of 10♥-10♣-9♥ for $300 and he calls. This is all part of the plan and I am happy as my hand is reasonably strong and he is loose so a medium strength hand is pretty good.

The turn is the 2♦ and I'm pretty sure my hand is best so I bet $700 here to get value and protect my hand, he calls. This is about the pot size I want to win with this strength of hand, as with a pot any bigger and I'll have to worry that he's been trapping me. The river is the 5♦, I check and he bets $550. Given the pot size it will be tough to fold here, especially given the first hand where he shows he makes bets that just don't make sense. I call and he has 10-8. There is nothing to be unhappy about here – it was a set up. He is a nutty player and he got a very good hand vs. my good hand, so it's inevitable that I'm going to lose money. In fact even though he won the hand I'm pretty happy as I could have easily lost more. He should have bet more on the river, and the board is draw heavy on straights and flushes so the fact that he wasn't aggressive with his good hand is promising. Rather than being upset about losing the pot I am excited about the rest of this match.

Hand 11

I open to $150 with J-6o and he calls. The idea is that since he plays bad pre-flop, I want to build the pot and take advantage of my position, and in my judgment he plays so bad that even raising with J-6o is profitable. He calls, the flop is 9♣-Q♦-10♥, he check-calls my $300 bet. The turn is the 4♦, he checks and I bet $900. My logic is again that he calls so much he could easily be weak and fold, and even if he calls it's okay because I probably have a good number of outs and vs. a player like this there are implied odds even though the draw is obvious. Also it allows me to maintain and build a quite aggressive image when in actuality it doesn't cost me much.

He calls, the river is the 2♦. This is a reasonable spot to bluff again. The factors to consider are that he is probably weak and I could easily have had a strong hand the whole way, but on the other hand he is loose. It's a close decision, and I have to be prepared for decisions like this when I play the way I did on the flop and turn. In the hand I checked and he checked behind with Q-7o. It's unclear what he would have done had I bet.

Hand 12

He opens to $150 and I fold J-7o. He is happy to play every pot I open out of position, so I'll focus on those pots and just try and play in position as much as I can.

Hand 13

I open to $150 with A-10o and he calls. The flop is A♦-9♠-J♥, he checks and I bet $300 – obviously versus this opponent I will not trap or slow-play. He check-raises to $600 and I'm not sure what that means exactly but I feel pretty good about my hand. The turn is the 8♦ and he checks. Time to make a decision here – he is bad but is he so bad that if I get all my money in here I am happy? I don't think so, and since I have a good draw it would be bad to bet the turn and have to fold. Also by checking and being deceptive there is a definite chance it could trap this player for value on the river whereas on the turn he'd fold. So I opted to check behind. The river is the Q♣, he checks I bet $1,050 and he called with A-3. Again his play is so bad and weird that it's unclear whether I should have bet the turn because he's so bad or if he just made the bad play because he got confused by the turn action.

Hand 14

His stack is $6,000 now and I cover. He raises to $150, I call with 6♥-5♥. The flop is 9♠-8♥-2♥, I lead out $300 into him because I'd rather keep the flop to one bet than two. If I check against this opponent there is a good chance he not only bets but he calls my check-raise which puts me in an awkward position for the turn, so I try to opt out of that by leading into him, and there's a good chance he'll call but my hand is so strong I don't lose much equity, and since I'm building the pot it's not bad at all.

The turn comes the 9♣, here I checked just because I didn't want to put more money in. However I didn't have a plan, and if I had taken the time to think out what my plan was I would have seen that had he bet I'd have to call, and there's a decent chance he'll bet here. Thus it makes more sense to just make the bet myself (and control the bet size), and also to gain some fold equity. The disadvantage is that he could raise which would be quite bad. And in the game that's why I didn't bet – I was afraid he had a 9 and would raise. In retrospect with more thought this fear seems unfounded based on how he played his previously. Earlier on when he had trip tens on the 10-10-9 board he called me twice without raising me. In contrast when he had top pair on the flop the A-3 vs. my A-10 hand he raised the flop. Both those factors lead to the idea that I need not be afraid of a turn raise.

I checked and he checked behind which was nice. The river is the 10♠ and now I have a decision to make. The timing on when he checked behind on the turn made me think he had an 8. The ten is a perfect scare card because the exact sort of hands people lead out on the 9-8-2 board are semi-bluffs like 10-Q, 10-J or 10-7. So I bet out $750 and he called with A-8. The fact that he would call there means my read on him and my play was bad, especially considering my read that he could have had a hand like 10-Q himself, and thus definitely call my river bluff. There are two parts to reading a person – first there is reading what hand they have, and next what they are likely to do with it. My ability to read him for A-8 is useless if I can't then read that he's going to call me when I bluff.

Hand 15

I raise to $150 with Q-4s, he reraises pot and I fold. Against someone like him I want to wait until I get a better hand to make a stand because not only will I be calling the pre-flop raise, if I want to go to showdown there is a good chance I'll need to invest a fair bit more. Also it appears as if there will be plenty of chances to play reraised pots with him pre-flop.

Hand 16

He raises to $150 and I fold J♥-2♥. Note the power of aggression. He keeps raising and reraising me and it works because this is HU and people don't get good hands often HU. Also note that his strategy of calling my bets a lot has worked for the same reason. It can be hard to play against someone who raises and calls a lot because HU you don't get hands often.

Hand 17

He now has $7,500 and I have $5,000. I raise to $150 with 9♥-7♥, he calls. The flop is 10♠-8♦-3♣, he check-calls a $250 bet. Turn is the J♠, he check-calls $750. River is the 9♦ and he checks. Well, he could have a queen, a seven, two pair or a set and there is no way of knowing. On the basis that he is bad and likes to call with bad hands, and also on the basis that he cannot bluff me here because it's so risky and perhaps reckless for him, I went ahead and made a thin and aggressive value bet of $1,750, which he promptly proceeded to min-raise and I folded.

Hand 18

He now has $10,000 and I of course immediately reload my stack to $5,000. He opens to $150 and I call with 9♥-J♥. The flop is 2♦-4♥-2♥, it goes check-check. Turn is the 3♠ and with my two overcard outs and flush outs I lead out $250, he calls. Since he didn't bet the flop I think he is floating me with a weak hand on the turn. The river comes the 6♦ which is a scary card for weak hands and overcards. Note how much easier this would be if my opponent was a predictable tight opponent – but he isn't, he's a loose unpredictable one who gives us tough decisions, like should we bluff here?

The 6♦ seemed like such a good card to do so, so I bet $625, and he called with 6♥-Q♥. So it turns out my read was right – he had some weird overcard hand not a good made hand, and he would have folded but he just happened to hit the river card which was impossible for me to know. This was an okay line and I just got unlucky. You should be evaluating all the hands to see who is outplaying who and if you should keep playing someone, if you should quit the game because they are outplaying you, or if they are bad but their style somehow matches up well against you and you just need to adjust.

Hand 19

I open to $150 with J♦-2♦, he reraises to $450, I fold. Now it's obviously time to really start adjusting my pre-flop play, and this perhaps should have been obvious to me the last time he reraised me but I will begin the adjustment now. Poker is a game of adjustments to opponents – if I had adjusted before this hand and realized I needed to tighten up pre-flop and limp and fold more against this opponent then I would have saved myself $150.

Hand 20

He opens to $150 and I fold K♦-2♥. This is standard, now my plan is to tighten up and just wait for good hands pre-flop and get value post-flop.

Hand 21

I open to $150 with A-Qo, he calls. Flop is 8♠-3♣-3♦, he checks and I bet $250 because my hand is probably best, and this opponent is bad enough to call me with worse. He calls, the turn is 8♣, check-check. The river is 7♥ and he leads out $550. Given my read and thoughts on the flop, and also that the board texture is extremely dry, it's quite hard for him to have hit that flop so I think there's a good chance my hand is best and that he called the flop to represent a hand later on. So I call, he has 6♣-9♣.

Hand 22

He has $11,000 and I have $5,700 now. He opens to $150 and I re-raise to $450 with A-A , he folds.

Hand 23

I open to $150 with 7-8o and he calls. The flop is 10♣-6♦-10♦, he checks and even though I have a lot of outs he calls so much that I can't really profitably bet here. The turn is the 8♥, he checks, and now my hand is almost surely good so I bet pot for value and he calls. The river is the 5♣, a good card in my opinion as I still think my hand is good so I bet as much as I think he'll call which is $700 and he calls with 6-3s.

Hand 24

He opens to $150, I fold 7♣-10♦. My strategy is to play hands in position.

Hand 25

I open to $150 with 8♠-4♠, he calls. The flop is 6♠-K♦-2♠, he checks and I want to build the pot or make him fold so I bet $300 and he calls. There are two reasons to bluff here – the combinations of him folding enough times to make it profitable and the times I outdraw him and the implied odds. The difference between this and hand 2-3 is that the implied odds are better (I'm comfortable playing a bigger pot with a flush then a pair of eights) and I have more outs.

He min-raises to $600 – not really sure what he has, but it's committing too much with a flush draw and no overcard to reraise him and get it all in so I call and the turn is the 8♥, he bets $650. After I call there will be about $3,100 in the pot. Semi-bluffing is a possibility here. I opted for less variance, wanted to hit my hand first and then get the money in later which is possible vs. bad players, plus my hand could very well be good so I called. The river is the 9♥ he checks and I check. He shows 10-Q and losses.

Hand 26

I fold 2-4o.

Hand 27

He raises to $150, I fold K-6o.

Hand 28

I fold 4-7o, normally I like to raise a lot pre-flop, regardless of my hand strength. And normally I can and do, but against this opponent I need to adjust and fold more.

Hand 29

He raises to $150, I fold K-2o. I can afford to play weak-tight pre-flop and give up equity because post-flop the opponent plays so bad and gives so much away there.

Hand 30

I limp with 4-8o. He checks, the flop is 10♥-9♠-2♠, he checks, I check. Turn is the 6♦, he bets $100 and I fold.

Hand 31

He raises to $150, I have 7♣-7♥. Reraising is a possibility for value and to mix it up but he is so loose it will be problematic to play post-flop. So I call, the flop is 2♣-6♠-6♣. At this point my hand is probably good, and he calls a lot so I lead out for $250. He calls, the turn is the J♣, there is no reason to think the jack hit him, and no reason to think he had a hand as strong as a flush draw so I bet again for $600, he calls. The river is the 8♣. I have a flush, but even against him this flush is too low to value bet. I check and he bets $850. The pot is $2,000. It looks like a value bet but given his history of making bets that make no sense it's a call because of the pot odds. He has 2♦-K♣ and wins. In retrospect there isn't much to regret though. We put $1,000 in when we were significantly ahead, then he got lucky

Hand 32

I raise to $150 with Q♥-J♥, he calls, the flop is 9♣-2♦-2♠. He checks, I check. The turn is the 9♠, he bets out $300 – it's not clear what he has but whenever I bet and raise he likes to call so I'll just wait until I have a hand and not bluff him here.

Hand 33

He raises to $150, I call with A-2o. The flop is K♥-3♠-3♥, I check he bets $300. Again will just wait until I get a hand because he likes to pay them off. I fold.

Hand 34

I raise the button to $150 with 8♥-9♥, he calls. The flop is Q♣-9♠-6♦, he checks and normally I'll check behind here with second pair for deception because generally only better hands call and worse hands fold or raise me out of the pot. However given the opponent's tendency to call, I value bet $250 and he raised to $750. He could be semi-bluffing but even if he is he has so many outs (with a hand like 10-K) that it's not worth it to call. I fold..

Hand 35

He raises to $150, I fold 4♦-7♠.

Hand 36

I raise to $150 with Q-J and he calls. The flop is A♦-8♦-A♥, check-check. The turn is the 5♦, he leads out $300 and I fold. Basically we are getting a cold deck here, and there is nothing to do but wait it out and lose as little as we can.

Hand 37

He raises to $150 and I have K-Qo. I reraise to $450 for value and to mix it up to disguise my better hands. He folds. He's folded the two times I have reraised him pre-flop, so I should start reraising him more to take advantage of his weakness there.

Hand 38

I raise to $150 with 9-8o, he calls. Flop is 2♠-6♠-7♦, and he leads out into me for $300. I'm not sure what that means with him. So I'll take a standard line here and raise him. Calling him is also reasonable. I raise to $1,000, the idea being that I've made the decision I am happy to go all in vs. him with my two overcards and open ended straight draw. Probably what will happen is he will call or fold. And if he calls then I can take a free card on the turn.

He calls, the turn is 2♣, he checks, I check. The river is 2♥, he bets $1,300 and I missed my draw, and there is no reason to think I can make a play here, and fold. Again we played fine but just didn't hit.

Hand 39

He raises to $150; I fold 3♦-Q♣.

Hand 40

I open to $150 with K♣-7♣, he calls. The flop is K♥-6♦-Q♦, I have top pair and will just value bet vs. this opponent. He folds, unfortunately. Some opponents are solid and if you bet with K-7 there you wouldn't even want a lot of action, but against this opponent we bet with the intention of getting action.

Hand 41

I fold 4-6o.

Hand 42

He raises to $150, I have 9-8o, and normally I'd call cause it's decent but strategically there is no reason. He calls all my bets when I'm on the button so I can just wait and only play those hands and my best hands OOP.

After this he leaves. What happened here is that the opponent was bad, but his style was quite different from most people and happened to match up well against how we played. It took too long to adjust, and we also made some imprecise plays and were unlucky. If he stayed forever that would be great, but alas he did not and thus we finished down over $5,000 to him.

Heads-up match #3, $25/50, $5,000 starting stacks

Hand 1

He opens to $150, I fold 6-9o.

Hand 2

I raise A-5o to $150, he folds.

Hand 3

He opens to $150, I fold 6-9o again.

Hand 4

I raise 6-8o to $150, he calls. The flop is A♦-Q♥-5♣, he checks and I bet $250. A check is reasonable too, especially given the board as opposed to if it was A-3-5 where it's less likely he has paired up. It's also possible he'll just fold his pair immediately. He called in the game. Turn is the 9♥, I just have a gutshot draw which isn't many outs to semi-bluff with, at this point I have pretty much given up on winning the pot. River comes a J♥ and he leads out $425, and given I have no read it is quite risky to try and bluff raise him so I fold

Hand 5

He raises to $150, I call with 8♣-Q♣, a standard call. The flop is A♣-10♦-2♦, I check, he bets $300 and I fold.

Hand 6

I raise J-3o to $150 and he folds.

Hand 7

He raises to $150 and I fold 9-2o.

Hand 8

I raise K-5o to $150, he folds.

Hand 9

He raises 2♥-8♦ to $150 and I fold. I've been playing pretty tight so far so I am looking to take advantage of that soon by reraising him pre-flop as a bluff.

Hand 10

I raise Q-10s to $150, he folds

Hand 11

He raises to $150 I fold 9-4o, I am tempted to raise but this hand is just too weak, especially against an unknown.

Hand 12

I limp with 8-6o, he checks. Flop is 2♣-9♠-K♥, he checks and I bet $75 as I would on any flop he checked to me. He folds.

Hand 13

He folds.

Hand 14

I open to $150 with K-3o, he calls. Flop is 10♣-3♦-4♥, he checks and I check. If I bet and he calls me I will not be happy and if he folds it won't help me too much so I check to see how things go. The turn is the 2♦, he leads out $300. This is a good board for him to semi-bluff with ace high, since he has the gutshot draw which gives him four additional outs. Since I checked the flop I think he could be bluffing or semi-bluffing so I call. The river is the 8♣, he leads out $425. On the turn I made a decision that I was probably ahead, but on the river I have no information, and his bet felt like he was value betting so I folded.

Hand 15

He folds..

Hand 16

I fold 3-8o.

Hand 17

He raises to $150 and I call with 10♦-9♣, which is standard. This hand deserves to be played HU. A reraise as a bluff is to be considered but he's won all the pots so far and when people are winning they can loosen up with their extra money and also play better, so that is a bad time to be reraise bluffing out of position with a marginal hand. The flop is 2♠-3♠-K♦, I check and he checks. The turn is the 4♠, this is a bad card to bluff because if he has ace high he can call now. If the turn was the 7♣ then to call with ace high he would have to think he's best a good amount of the time. Now he can think that he has the best hand a little bit of the time and the other times that he can outdraw me. So I check, he checks. The river is the 7♣, I'm not sure what he has now – I think it could be nothing but in this situation I don't really need to risk a lot to bluff. If he has any pair at all he might call a full pot bet because we checked all the previous streets. If he has a high card he will probably fold to me, and fold to any bet at all. A big bet isn't necessary vs. him if he just has a jack high, queen high, and maybe ace high. So I bet $50, he folded.

Hand 18

I raise to $150 with 10-6o, he calls. The flop is J♠-K♥-6♦, he checks, and I check too. If he calls I'm probably beat. The turn comes the 3♦. He leads out $200, this bet could be any sort of made hand, his hand range is wide here. Since his hand range is wide and not strong this is a good opportunity to bluff raise him. There are also draws on this board, so a few things could happen here. He could call me with a strong made hand, like a pair of kings. He could fold a weaker made hand like a pair of jacks. Or he could call me with a straight or flush draw. If he calls me with a draw that is good because he doesn't have pot odds – he thinks he has implied odds but he really doesn't because we aren't giving him any more action. The problem with this play arises in a couple of cases – first when we misjudged his hand range and he has a strong hand a lot of the time or when he calls us with a weak made hand a lot of the time. In this case he folded.

Hand 19

He raises to $150 and I have K♦-10♠ and reraise to $500. Raising to $500 here in itself is probably a breakeven play more or less, but I want to ensure that he gives me action when I reraise with a good hand. The reason I raised to $500 and not $450 is I wanted to try and get him to fold, but he calls (which isn't really too bad). The flop is 10♦-Q♠-4♥, I check and he checks.

The turn is the 5♠, it seems like my hand is best and there are a fair number of cards that are bad for me – a nine, a jack, or an ace. Not only that but on the flop if I checked and he bet there's a decent chance I'd just fold. However on the turn since he checked behind on the flop there is more doubt in my mind (and less streets to build a pot and force me out) so I am willing to put a bet into the pot. I have to decide what is better, to check-call or to bet and get called. Betting and getting called is a better way to get money into the pot so I do. He calls, the river is the A♥.

This is an interesting spot to bet because after he calls the turn there is a fair chance he has a pair of queens. It could be A-Q in which case he is calling my bet, but it could also be Q-K or Q-J or even Q-9 in which case he folds. Even if he has a hand like A-J that was peeling the flop lightly because he thought he might be ahead and even if he wasn't he could outdraw me, he will have a hard time calling. He'll have a hard time calling because I'll bet close to the pot at about $2,300 and also because after I reraised pre-flop and bet so big on such a high coordinated board that is showing a lot of strength, and it's completely consistent and believable. In the end though I decided not to bluff because my hand could be good now, and if it isn't my bluff is mainly to make him fold a pair of queens

However after further consideration a bet is best because there is little downside since his hand range is so wide and weak. He could have a pocket pair J-J or below tens that can't call my bet or wouldn't be able to bluff me. He can have a straight draw or flush draw and if he had the flush draw with ace high there is very little chance he can call my bet – the only thing he has that is good is the

K-J but that is just one hand. A-4 and A-5 which would give him two pair he probably folds pre-flop or on the turn. A-Q gives us trouble but there are less hand combinations of A-Q than there are of Q-K, and we can also combine Q-K and Q-J to give us a lot more combos of pairs of queens he could have that will fold the river instead of call.

After I checked he bet $825, apparently a small value bet from a small made hand like A-K, A-J or A-x with a flush draw. It could be a big hand making a small bet to be tricky and gain value but as we already established from hand reading it's hard for him to have two pair. It's probably not a pair of queens going for a thin value bet, as it takes a special kind of player to make such an aggressive value bet and they are not too common. He could also have some random hand that is impossible to put him on. Given that we're getting such good pot odds of 3:1 a call is justified. Although given his hand ranges it makes sense to check-raise all-in because a likely hand for him to have is a bare pair of kings, and given the scary board and our reraise pre-flop and turn bet, it would look strong. However I ended up folding because I had vague worries about him value betting a pair of queens, and if that's true it widens his hand range significantly and makes it a fold. But after thinking things through it's clear he isn't betting a queen so I should have at least called. He showed 7-6s.

Hand 20

It's important now to tilt as little as possible. He might think we are tilting so we should take advantage of that by making thinner value bets. Also the fact that he would underbet bluff the river there and show a bluff is a bad play and it made me lose respect for the opponent so I will adjust accordingly. I have K-Jo and raise to $150, he calls. Flop is K♣-10♦-Q♦, he check-folds when I bet $300, my hand was pretty good so I wanted value.

Hand 21

He folds. Sometimes people loosen up after winning because they have a big stack and don't realize the value of the money anymore since there is so much, and sometimes they tighten up to protect their winnings. This is an indication he is tightening up but we will learn more soon.

Hand 22

I raise to $150 with K-6o, he calls. The flop is 8♦-5♣-J♥, he checks and I check. The turn is the 4♠, he checks and I check. The river is the 9♠, he bets $175, kind of suspicious but I'm not sure, and without a read bluffs are bad so I fold.

Hand 23

He limps, I check with 4♠-9♣, the flop is A♠-4♥-5♦, I check fold to his $100. Just because I hit something doesn't mean I need to continue – it's a weak made hand with not many outs (if I'm behind), and I'm out of position.

Hand 24

I raise to $150 with 8-6o, he folds.

Hand 25

He raises to $150, I fold 4-5o.

Hand 26

I fold 4-2o.

Hand 27

He folds.

Hand 28

I raise 4♣-9♣ to $150, he calls. The flop is A♦-10♥-Q♠, he checks and he checked so fast it felt like he was just hurrying to get to the next hand cause he had nothing, so I bet $250, he folded.

Hand 29

He raises to $150, I fold 10-6o.

Hand 30

I raise to $150 with Q♥-7♥, he calls. The flop is 2♦-10♥-2♠, he checks and I check. Since I've raised pre-flop a fair amount I think he will be suspicious of me on a board like 2-2-10 since it is so uncoordinated it's unlikely I hit. The turn is the 6♦, he leads out $300 and I fold, not much I can do there.

Hand 31

He raises to $150 and I fold J-3o

Hand 32

Now he has $7,000 and I have $5,000. I raise to $150 with 4♠-5♠ and he folds.

Hand 33

He raises to $150 and I have 10-4o and fold. It's about time to reraise him again to mix it up but we need some semblance of a hand.

Hand 34

I raise 8-6o to $150, he folds.

Hand 35

He folds.

Hand 36

I fold 4♠-10♣. It would be quite easy to raise here with the mindset of "I'm here to win money" But I'm playing to simply play the game of poker and play the game as best I can. Sometimes when playing the game as best I can I have to lose money, as if I'm getting bad cards I can't force myself to win money – it doesn't work like that. I just have to keep playing my best and be proud of that, and as a result money will come.

Hand 37

He folds.

Hand 38

I raise 4♠-9♠ to $150. The way I like to break people down is by applying pressure to them, annoying them, and forcing them to fight back and do something. He calls, the flop is 5♥-7♠-Q♣, he checks and I check. The turn is the 10♥, he bets $300 and I fold. That is okay, if he is going to bet all the turns after I check the flop I can adjust.

Hand 39

He folds.

Hand 40

I fold 2-9o.

Hand 41

He raises to $150, I have 10-10. Calling is reasonable and so is raising, but I choose raise because I almost certainly have the best hand, and since he called me before when I reraised thought he'd call again. He folded.

Hand 42

I raise to $150 with Q-8o, he folds.

Hand 43

He raises to $150, I reraise to $450 with 9-9. I reraised because my hand is almost certainly better than his hand. Also because I am not afraid of playing this person out of position with a tricky hand like 9-9. He calls, the flop comes K♠-Q♣-Q♦, I check and he checks. There is not much for me to accomplish with a bet. The turn is the 7♥, I check and he checks, again there is not much for me to do with a bet. The river is the A♠, I check he checks and mucks 6-7s. Note how vs. a good player we would have lost this pot (and also how our reraise preflop would have created problems for us post-flop) but against. him we won money and had no problems. That should make us happy to be in this game. This hand is a good example of where we just won $450 not because of how the cards happened to fall, but because we play better than our opponent and we earned the $450. Now we have good momentum which means I will play better and he will play worse.

Hand 44

I raise to $150 with A-8o, he calls. The flop is Q♠-K♦-3♥, we both check. The turn is the 10♦ and he leads out $200. He keeps leading out when I check behind the flop and he can't always have a good hand, also he bet less here than normal which could be weakness, and also we have outs, so I chose here to semi-bluff raise pot to $900. He folded.

Hand 45

He raises to $150, I fold K-4o.

Hand 46

I limp with 2-5s, he raises to $150 and since I have the momentum and am playing good and have position I call – if it wasn't suited I would fold. The flop is 2♣-J♠-3♦, he bets $300. I have position, a pair and am not convinced that he has anything so I call the $300. The turn is the 5♥ and he leads out $450. We have two pair which HU is quite a strong hand, but still he bet just $450 and we both have $5,000 left so if we are going to get it all-in that is a lot more, and also our two pair is a low two pair. We have to decide if we are happy to get it all-in here. Given that he doesn't seem to be too skilled an opponent, and that it's a little hard to put him on a better hand it would be okay to get all in. Also our hand is quite vulnerable, so I raised to $1,700 and he folded.

Hand 47

He folds.

Hand 48

I raise to $150 with 8-10, he folds. I have $7,000 and he has $5,000.

Hand 49

He folds.

Hand 50

I open to $150 with 5-Qo, he reraises to $450 and I fold.

Hand 51

He raises to $150. I fold K-9 (which I wouldn't normally do but my computer crashed!).

Hand 52

He folds.

Hand 53

I fold 3-2o.

Hand 54

He raises to $150, I fold 3-6s. HU big cards are good and small suited cards don't have that much value. HU a bad strategy is to call pre-flop with speculative hands and hope they hit and hope you get a lot of money into the pot when they hit – because most of the time they won't hit and you will just have to fold and lose your pre-flop investment. In HU hold'em if you are going to loosen up pre-flop you have to also loosen up post-flop and fight for more pots.

Hand 55

I raise to $150 with 8-6s, he folds.

Hand 56

He raises to $150. I fold 10-7.

Hand 57

I raise to $150 with Q-6, he reraises to $450, I fold. I've been opening a lot pre-flop so his last two reraises of me were good skillful adjustments by him which cost me some money.

Hand 58

He folds.

Hand 59

I fold 5-2o.

Hand 60

He raised to $150, and I called with 7♣-9♣. I check and he bets $300 on a board of 9♦-5♠-5♣. Normally I would call because it's not that strong of a hand but since the board was so dry I thought a raise might be deceptive and look like a bluff. In retrospect I probably just wanted to mix it up and build a big pot because I was bored from all the inaction. He called, which was my plan, but really it is a suspect plan. My standard line of calling is good for a reason, and there's a reason why I almost always do it instead of raising. The reason is that my hand isn't that good and once he calls me I can't be too happy.

The turn comes the 5♥, I check and he bets $525. My hand is decently strong and with those pot odds a call is quite reasonable. He could have a pair of nines, some wacky bluff or a low pocket pair protecting his hand and going for a free showdown on the river. I called, the river is the Q♦, I check and he bets $2,400. Given the inaction in the game so far, and the fact that I'm still down $500, I really wanted to call to win a pot and to see a showdown and almost did.

Fortunately however I took some time to think it through. He called my flop bet and then made a small value bet on the turn then bet big on the river. That is basically him showing strength, and my hand is quite mediocre. It's quite possible he has a pocket pair above nines, and even possible he has quad fives because the flop wasn't 5-5-5, so it's more likely he has a 5 in his hand. Also his turn bet makes sense with a five because his hand is so strong he is trying to get any action he can, unafraid of any cards that come. I folded and he won the pot.

Hand 61

I raise to $150 with K-2o, he calls. The flop is K♥-K♦-3♠, he check-folds to a $250 bet. Checking is reasonable too. Note that we don't flip a coin to randomize the decision so we become "unreadable" and "unexploitable" by the opponent. Since we are better than the opponent we out-think him and keep adding in pieces of information and analysis until we can decide which is a better play in this specific hand.

Hand 62

He folds.

Hand 63

I fold 10-3o.

Hand 64

He raises to $150, I call with 2-2. The flop is A♣-Q♥-4♣, I check, he checks. The turn is the J♦, I check, he bets $300, I fold. The board is so coordinated and my hand is so weak this is an easy fold.

Hand 65

I raise to $150 with J-9o, he calls. The flop is 2♦-A♣-10♥, he checks, I bet $300, he folds. Its good to continuation bet bluff some of the time.

Hand 66

I have Q♣-10♣, he raises to $150 and I reraise to $475, he folds. It's okay if he folds or calls and it's also an okay play for me to flat call. I reraised here because he plays bad, so I'd rather him play bad with me in a big reraised pot than in a small pot so I can win more money faster.

Hand 67

I raise to $150 with Q-7o, he folds.

Hand 68

He folds. Now I have $6,700 and he has $5,300.

Hand 69

I fold 2-8o.

Hand 70

He folds.

Hand 71

I fold 9-3o.

Hand 72

He folds.

Hand 73

I limp with A♦-9♥ to mix it up. He was losing and we had just played a lot of small pots so I thought he might get frustrated when I limped and raise me, and then I could reraise him with position. He checked. The flop is 10♣-8♠-K♥, he checks, I check. The turn is the J♥. He bets $100, I fold.

Hand 74

He folds..

Hand 75

I raise A-Qo to $150, he folds.

Hand 76

He raises to $150, I call with 10-8 – it's not the best hand but I haven't called many of his raises so he should give my call a little respect which will give me room to manoeuvre post-flop. The flop is 5♦-4♠-4♣, I check, he checks behind. The turn is the J♠ and this is my opportunity to try and take it after he checked, so I bet $275 and he calls. Maybe he hit a pair of jacks – that is most likely and it will be very unlikely that I can push him off it so I pretty much give up on the hand at this point. The river is the 2♦, I check fold to his $450 bet.

Hand 77

I raise 5♦-9♦ to $150, he calls. The flop is 4♥-6♠-J♠, we both check. The turn is the K♦, he checks. He kept betting when I checked on the flop, so now he doesn't bet I interpret it as him having no hand so I bluff $300 and he folds. Unless he has a pair of jacks or kings it's hard for him to call and given his history of betting out on the turn so much it seems like he would lead out with kings or jacks.

Hand 78

He folds.

Hand 79

I win with a raise to $150 with 9♠-2♠.

Hand 80

He raises to $150, I fold K-7o.

Hand 81

I fold 6-2o.

Hand 82

He folds.

Hand 83

I raise to $150 with A-K. he calls. The flop is 7♣-K♦-7♥. Some people always bet here, and a smaller group of people always check here. Some people might say flipping a coin to randomize is the best thing to do but none of them are right. The best player first of all adjusts to his opponent and for some opponents a bet is better here, and for some a check is better. And they also adjust to how the game has been playing lately to make this decision. Versus this opponent a check is probably better since he seems to bet out on the turn so much. If an opponent doesn't bluff often it's better to just bet the flop and try and get value. Some opponents are smart and if they have J-10 and hit a pair of tens on the turn won't lose a lot of money because they will see our flop check for what it was, a trap. Others will lose money. These are some factors to consider in whether to bet or check here. I bet, but that was an impatient mistake – as I said since he bets out on the turn so much this is a good spot to check..

Hand 84

He raises to $150, I fold 4-10o.

Hand 85

I fold Q-2o.

Hand 86

He raises to $150, I fold 5-6o. He's playing okay poker but I can out-wait him. Also he played bad in our one big pot earlier and it's only a matter of time before he does the same again.

Hand 87

I raise 5♣-9♠ to $150, he calls. The flop is J♣-6♥-7♣, he checks, I check. The turn is the 9♣, he checks, I check. A reason not to bet here is because our hand could be good and because we have draws and if he raises us on this sort of drawy board it could be a semi-bluff. However this opponent seems to be quite passive. Because of that fact a bet should be considered to gain value against worse made hands and draws or combinations of the two, and to prevent him bluffing me on the river, and also we then have flexibility in how we play the river if he calls us and has a better hand. However I didn't think through all that and just checked which is my standard play. The river is the 3♦, he led out $300 and I folded. This is a close decision but he doesn't have a history of bluffing a lot so I folded – it's important to play precise poker and save these small to medium sized bets when possible.

Hand 88

He folded.

Hand 89

I fold 9-2o.

Hand 90

He folds. Now I have $7k and he has $5k.

Hand 91

I fold 4-3o.

Hand 92

He raises to $150, I call with K♣-5♣, this is a standard call as K-xs is a decent hand. The flop is K♥-7♣-4♣ I check, he checks. The turn is the 5♠, this is a good time to check. I want to get as much money into the pot as I can and after I check two times it becomes more tempting for him to bet. The board is kind of coordinated so he can bet the turn with a lot of made hands, draws, and combos of them both.

And when I check-raise given the drawy nature of the board he won't know whether I have a made hand or am semi-bluffing.

I check, he bet $300 and I check-raised the pot to $1,200 which he called. The river is the 9♣, so now it's time to bet as much as I think he'll call. which felt like $2,400 He called with K-9, and made a bad play by calling my turn check-raise. He got tricked by my play and should have just folded as he's either behind or I have a lot of outs.

Hand 93

I fold J-6o. Now I have $8,200, he has $3,200.

Hand 94

He raises to $150, I fold 10♥-3♥.

Hand 95

I limp with 5♣-7♦, I thought he might be steaming and more likely to call my raise or reraise me and 5-7o isn't a good hand to deal with those possibilities. He checked. The flop is 7♥-5♦-2♦, he bet $100. It felt like he had nothing so I wanted to let him hang himself and just called. Raising the flop is the standard play, as there are straight and flush draws that both outdraw us and also ruin our action. But the reason I just called was because he was probably steaming and had nothing and if he had absolutely nothing just calling is the right play. The turn is the Q♥ and he check-folds.

Hand 96

He raises to $150, I fold Q-4o.

Hand 97

I raise 9-9 to $150, he folds.

Hand 98

He raises to $150, I fold J-4o.

Hand 99

I raise K-10o to $150, he folds.

Hand 100

He raises to $150, I have A-A . Normally this is a reraise but given that he has raised every hand since losing the big pot and is apparently tilting, he probably does not have a hand so it's unclear what he'll do against a reraise (probably fold). Also since he is tilting he will probably commit too much to a pot post-flop with one pair hands or top pair hands. So I just called.

The flop is A♣-9♦-10♦, I check and he checks. The turn is the 2♥ and I lead out. A check-raise might be a nice play here but it's pretty risky that he'll check behind pairs of tens and nines that he might call my bet with. Also he'd fold those to a check-raise which is bad, so we just bet out. He calls and the river is the A♦. From his perspective this is a mixed card – it makes it less likely we hold an ace but it does make the flush which is something we could have had. There is nothing we can do here but bet and hope he calls. I bet $750 and he called with K-10o, so clearly he is tilting.

Hand 101

I open 10-Jo to $150, he reraises me to $450, and strategically there is no reason to force marginal situations now. He is playing very bad. I don't want to let him double up and then he will start playing better. It's much better here to play tight and wait for a clear winning situation. I folded.

Hand 102

He folds.

Hand 103

I fold 5-2o. Now he has $2k and I have $10,000.

Hand 104

He raises to $150, I fold K-7o

Hand 105

I raise J♥-Q♥ to $150, he folds.

Hand 106

He raises to $150, I fold 3-6o.

Hand 107

I raise 8♣-6♣ to $150, he folds.

Hand 108

He folds.

Hand 109

I fold 4-6o.

Hand 110

He raises to $150, I call with A-5o. It's reasonable to fold this hand pre-flop, but here I call since he's playing bad, and also since he only has 40 big blinds that will make our decisions easier if we hit top pair. I call, the flop is 4♥-2♣-8♠, I check, he checks. The turn is the 3♣. I don't think he's calling, and if he has nothing I want to give him the chance to hit something, and if he has something a check-raise line here is nice too for trying to win more money. He checks behind, the river is the 3♠. It doesn't seem like he has anything to call my bet. So I tried to trap him for a bluff again, or if he did have something I can check-raise and he will probably call which is key to this play, since our check-raise looks so suspicious. Unfortunately he checked behind with ace high. That is a hand we missed value in as he probably was calling a turn bet with his two overcards and straight outs, and also he might have even called the river on such a dry board with ace high.

Hand 111

I raise to $150 with 10-8o, he folds.

Hand 112

He raises to $150, I call with Q-K. It's reasonable to raise but if he goes all-in (which is relatively easy for him because of his stack size) things are awkward for me. Also vs. this bad opponent a low variance approach is good so he doesn't get a chance to get even and play better or leave. The flop is Q♣-8♣-J♥, this is a good situation to win all of his remaining $2,000. I have a good hand, good enough to go all-in with and the board is coordinated so he can have lesser hands. There are a lot of hands here that will check behind on the flop like a pair of jacks or eights, or a pair and a gutshot straight draw, or an overcard and gutshot straight draw so I bet out $250 and he called.

The turn is the 6♠ and there is no way to trap him really, although in a way we have by betting out on the flop when he is tilting and a lot of the time people lead with semi-bluffs. If we check here it makes a lot of sense for him to check behind with all of the hands we want to gain value against so we just have to bet out again and have him make a decision. So I bet $800 and he went all-in, and I called obviously. He had A-J and lost his last money.